Beguiling

Beguiling Burma

Awe and wonder on the road to Mandalay

PATRICK FORSYTH

RƎTHINK PRESS

First Published as "A Land Like None You Know"
in Thailand 2008 by Bangkok Books

This fully revised edition Published in Great Britain 2012
by Rethink Press (www.rethinkpress.com)

Cover image of the famous, timber U Bein Bridge
© Colleen Kerrigan www.istockphoto.com/chk959

For Anna (without you ...)
and, of course, Sue too (ditto).

"... quite unlike any land you know about ..."
Rudyard Kipling
(who visited Burma a century ago)

Author's Note

Burma is a fascinating and beautiful country; the "beguiling" of the title here seems to me to be wholly appropriate. By describing my particular journey, I hope to create a snapshot that casts some light on a for-too-long-hidden country and people. Though largely leaving the politics on one side and taking a light-hearted approach, I hope to act to help create amongst readers an interest in a special place: one that deserves not just the admiration of others but our help too.

The other word I should use as you begin to follow my journey is "dynamic". That surely applies to Burma in the full meaning of the word. Change is needed, but some change is happening and since I wrote this book a bewildering series of events and changes have occurred: further anti-government protests have taken place and, while the world was shocked by pictures of peaceful monks being shot in the crackdown, very little international weight was thrown about as a result.

In addition, the cyclone Negris, reportedly the worst natural disaster in Burma's recorded history, hit the river delta killing, injuring or taking the homes of hundreds of thousands of people while the government again showed its true colours through their inadequate response. Since then certain tentative steps towards a more democratic regime have been made, with some (though very few) political prisoners being released and some seeming relaxations being made to the government's stranglehold on the population

This shift may be no more than a small step in the right direction, but there is hope that more will follow. Those who have, in the past, campaigned to encourage people *not* to visit Burma (because of the support doing so is regarded as, albeit unwittingly, giving to the government) have recently relaxed their stance and it is increasingly the case that travel to the country is being encouraged. I do touch on this later, but it seems that the moment when this book is appearing is timely. Many people want to know more about Burma, and I aim to play a small part with that, but also a greater number of people are likely to visit.

I believe that this increase may change things still more; as you will see, I certainly hope so.

Contents

Prologue

"To have a grievance is to have a purpose in life"
Eric Heffer

Antidote time.

There were two reasons for me undertaking the journey described here: one was an old song – and the other was an objectionable man called Harold.

Harold sat next to me on a long-haul flight to Singapore. He was two sizes too big for the meagre economy seat and he announced as he sat down, or rather collapsed into the seat from a great height, "I'm going to make your flight hell," and he did.

Who was it that said, "Hell is other people"? Whoever it was, they probably had to fly economy. Of course, flying is a modern marvel. Turn up at the airport and a few hours later you can be on the other side of the world. Wonderful. Well, provided you ignore the journey to the airport, the queues, security checks and general angst that pervades the process of actually getting onto a plane it is. And sometimes the flight itself can be a relatively tolerable experience; certainly it is better than the months on a boat to get to say Australia, which people had to suffer in the years of sailing ships. But, and it's a big but, there is much about the whole process that can be miserable: the seats are too small, the food is dire, the time change on long haul flights adds another hazard to surmount and you need a holiday when you get to the other end just to recover and get ready for your holiday.

I was brought up by the sea and travelled little as a child. When I was young, I thought going down to the beach hut we had below a small cliff a couple of hundred yards from the house was a holiday. Going to the Channel Islands as a teenager was a great adventure and I remember going abroad for the first time on business in my early twenties being very daunting. "I don't speak any French," I told my boss before leaving to attend a conference in Nice. "No matter," he replied, "I'll write down what you need to be able to say." When I looked at his note on the plane it set out the French for two phrases: the first was, *May I have a beer, please?* And the second was, *My friend will pay.* For years since then, just like most people, I guess, all my travel has been conditioned by a budget. Whenever I face the prospect of the costs involved, certainly of travelling long haul, it brings on an attack of my IBS – that's irritable bank syndrome.

Many of us balance where we go, and how long we stay with the cost. Most trips involve compromise, and despite the large costs involved I work at reducing other costs in a vain attempt to make a trip seem reasonable. Consider doing your laundry when you are away. A large hotel will charge a substantial amount, enough to make you wonder whether to have a clean shirt or another beer. In Thailand, which I have visited often, there is a little laundry near my favourite hotel, which will do the entire accumulated laundry of two people from a week's travelling for the cost of not much more than a pint of beer. Collecting my laundry from there on one occasion it was presented neatly wrapped as always, but without the laundry bag I had used to bring it in. The laundry lady produced a large pile of such drawstring bags and sorted through them all to find mine. Every single one was from a select hotel: Shangri-La, Mandarin Oriental, and others; and I bet that, like mine, they had all been taken to compensate for high laundry prices. Though, in my defence, I have had mine for many years going back to a time when they were a give away item. Really.

Despite everything to do with cost I decided, just for once and as an antidote to a lifetime's travel nightmares, to blow the budget and set up a trip on a wholly different basis: going first class in every way. It was a revelation. The journey was truly wonderful (and I wrote about it in my book *First class at last!*), but it was all too soon over and my subsequent journeys were arranged, as before, with due deference to costs, even those necessary to keep my shirts in pristine condition. However, I had been spoiled now and after my one truly exceptional journey I found I resented all the various economy class discomforts even more than in the past.

And then I came across Harold.

It was when I was going to Singapore on business. I was travelling in what a friend of mine calls scum class. For ten minutes as people boarded the plane the seat next to mine had remained tantalisingly empty. I was by the window, and a woman of uncertain age was ensconced in the aisle seat reading a copy of *The Lady*. She looked unlikely to drink too much or play loud rock music that would spill out of her iPod into the surrounding air. She looked more likely to get out her knitting. There was not a baby in sight either - so far so good.

At that stage of the boarding process it is always almost impossible not to harbour the impossible dream of having an empty seat next to you. You watch everyone coming down the aisle willing them to walk on past. Other passengers in your immediate area can help make a flight tolerable or turn it into something worse than a day trip to Hades. On other forms of transport it is possible to make some attempt to fend off people intent on sitting next to you. On a train or bus say, the best tactic is not, as people sometimes believe, to pile baggage of some sort on the seat alongside you. The kind of people you want to discourage, and send on past you down the aisle, will always take a perverse delight in making you move it. A better approach is to leave the seat empty. Then, as someone approaches it, you flash a maniacal smile at them and pat the seat next to you encouragingly. No one wants to sit next to the nutter on the bus and so, doubting your sanity, they tend to pass you by. But on a plane, seats are usually pre-allocated, certainly on scheduled and long haul flights. The battle for seats on a "free seating" budget airline is another matter, and another horror. But if someone has been allocated the seat number next to you then they will almost certainly sit in it and there is precious little you can do about it. Keeping your fingers crossed or praying to some imagined seat selection god is sadly vanishingly unlikely to make any difference.

If you are unlucky then you can be stuck with the source of that bad luck for many hours. Even a small thing can add to the unavoidable irritations in a big way. Someone who has had too much to drink or talks incessantly, the kind of premature articulation that won't let you get a word in even to say shut up, can be a nightmare. On one occasion I sat near a woman with a piercing, raucous and uncouth voice, who punctuated every phrase with "like"; a minor disturbance perhaps, but over time it soon became maddening. My quiet neighbour and I raised eyebrows and exchanged glances at one point when her latest outburst ended in a shriek of laughter and he said, "Just think, that must be the first sound the poor guy with her hears every morning". Right: there's always someone worse off than you are, and that's actually not such a bad thought to keep in mind when you are flying.

So, as these thoughts and reminiscences ran through my mind, my designated fellow traveller lurched into view. He was carrying a ridiculous amount of baggage, with his various odd-shaped parcels brushing the heads of people already seated as he passed. He dumped half of them across the lady in the aisle seat who looked as horrified as I felt, then leant to and fro to retrieve them and put them into the overhead locker. He was both ordinary, yet at the same time threatening. His face shone with sweat and so, my nose soon discovered, did his armpits. Aged about forty and already dressed for the beach, his long Bermuda shorts were of a curtain material favoured by those with neither taste nor a need for sunglasses. His shirt was coming adrift from his shorts, a process made worse by several buttons being undone, and a section of his large stomach was visible. He looked as if he kept a bulldog and ran a tattoo parlour. He didn't actually say he was going to make my flight hell, of course, but his demeanour spoke unmistakable volumes.

He flopped into his seat, said "Good morning, I'm Harold," planted his left elbow firmly in my ribs, his earphones in his ears and called the cabin attendant demanding a drink even while other passengers continued to board the plane. The attendant whose eye he had caught smiled back at him, but her eyes flashed a look that could have burnt holes in the aircraft's hull. "Listen you ignorant lout," she said, "Just wait and be quiet until we are in the air then I might get you something, though only if your behaviour improves markedly and remains good throughout the flight." Sadly, of course, she said no such thing, just murmured sweetly that she would be back as soon as possible. But I wished that she had said something that fierce and so did the aisle lady, I am sure.

None of this boded well, and some hours on, as my attempts at sleep were constantly thwarted by his moving, snorting, breaking wind and the buzz of some primitive rhythm issuing from whatever music player was tucked into his shirt pocket, my worst fears were surpassed. It was the longest flight of my life. I read recently that astronomers have announced the discovery of the most Earth-like exoplanet yet. It orbits the memorably named star Gliese 581, and is itself catchily named HD 69830d. It is more than 120 trillion miles away in the direction of the Libra constellation, and orbits just the right distance from its sun to be able to support life. They reckon there is water on it. It is a bit larger than the Earth, so that gravity would be greater and a great step for mankind there would take a fair old effort. Still, the item I read in the newspaper actually quoted one Xavier Delfosse of Grenoble University as saying, "... this planet will most probably be a very important target of the future space missions dedicated to the search for extraterrestrial life." When I read this I thought that surely the distance ruled out any thoughts about going there, however much fun it might be to meet any 69830dlings living there, certainly until something is invented to make a simple journey like going to Singapore a bit easier. Now looking back on that Singapore flight, I reckon I'll sign up for the space flight, the journey time would surely seem to be as nothing compared with a trip with Harold.

As he pumped his elbows yet again I made a decision. I would organise another exceptional trip, one that took me away from all this sort of thing and was again exceptional all the way. Harold still made that flight a miserable one, but I tried to ignore his ever moving elbow and dwelt on my decision to plan another special trip; doing so did make me feel a little better.

What I had to do next was to decide where in the world I should go. As the flight time went slowly by, I watched a dire movie and then turned over to one of the music channels, more to keep my earphones in and Harold out of my consciousness than because I wanted to listen to music. The music playing as I switched on was an easy listening selection, which for the most part meant easily ignored and easily forgotten, but one track did grab my attention. Frank Sinatra launched into the song *Road to Mandalay*.

On the road to Mandalay,
Where the flying fishes play,
And the dawn comes up like thunder,
Out of China cross the bay.

It is an old standard, featured originally I think on his album *Come fly with me*, so perhaps appropriately being played to me at 30,000 feet. The words were sort of familiar, not least because the song is derived from a poem written by Rudyard Kipling, titled simply *Mandalay*, which is in fact written from the viewpoint of an old soldier, back from the wars and remembering his time in the exotic place.

A few minutes slipped by as I half listened to this, my mind roamed somewhat and I found myself asking "Mandalay. Wherever is that?" But I also found I couldn't answer my own question with any certainty. The song spoke of pagodas and contained the line "China cross the bay" - presumably indicating that the place was in the East but, although it was a place the name of which I knew, I found I could not place it. I snoozed and when I stirred – Harold was on the move again – I found that the music programme had gone full circle and reached the same song again. This time I took in another line in the lyrics: *From Rangoon to Mandalay.* Rangoon I did know: that was the capital of Burma, a country lying just north and west of Thailand, and Thailand was a country that I had visited many times*. Mandalay suddenly sounded exotic and mysterious and it had to be somewhere nearby.

It sounded good. I had already decided to set up another trip as an antidote to being Haroldised. To this intention I now added an intriguing destination – I decided I would go to Burma to visit exotic Mandalay, and I would do so in some style. I was adamant. The only thing that would put me off would be to discover that Harold had the same intention. He had finally lapsed into a deep and noisy sleep so I could not ask him, but I hoped it was unlikely.

Some days later, that flight over and consigned to be forgotten before it put me off ever wanting to travel again, and on my return to England with my resolve still firm, I set about finding out more and making arrangements for the trip. Would my initial feeling that Mandalay was an irresistible destination hold up in the cold light of day, or was my idea as doomed as my attempts to pretend that Harold was not making every moment of my flight miserable?

———

* Details of my travels in Thailand can be found in the book entitled *Smile Because it Happened*

Chapter One

A FEARFULLY GOOD IDEA

"Dangers bring fears, and
fears more dangers bring."
Richard Baxter

Having established that Mandalay is in Burma, I did a little research to give me a more precise picture. Knowing other parts of South East Asia to some extent, I certainly knew of Burma. My knowledge though was not in any way detailed, but more random. For example, I did know that Burmese cats are not Burmese but come from Thailand, not that that is vital information to making a visit to either country. If I was to make another special trip it had to be a good choice of destination. I bought a guidebook. The *Insight Guide* was the first one I chose, partly because it looked beautifully illustrated and partly because I found a second hand copy of the latest edition on Amazon's web site. I was not into major spending just yet. It arrived as promised and had the word Burma on the cover, with the word Myanmar in smaller type. In 1989 the Burmese Government changed the name of the country. What was officially called the Union of Burma became the Union of Myanmar. This was a move made not without considerable contention; it is said that it was part of an attempt to rewrite history and have many events from the past forgotten. Still the name Burma hangs on and remains in use with perhaps most people around the world, so I will use it here, just as the *Insight* guide does.

Scanning only a few pages showed that the country looked both beautiful and fascinating. The guide referred to its "eternal beauty", it called it "magical" and even a cursory glance at the photographs seemed to demonstrate their point. They showed temples, rolling countryside, unspoiled looking towns and villages, elephants, markets, temples, smiling faces – many covered with patches of *thanaka*, a sandalwood paste traditionally used to protect the skin from the sun - spectacular sunsets, river scenes and one more thing ... yet more temples.

I found that this was a country with history and tradition going back thousands of years, a turbulent history with wars aplenty and, like so many parts of the world, with a period spent under British colonial rule. A "land of gold" populated by "a deeply religious and dignified people," *Insight* said and, by the look of it, with more temples than Britain has parking meters. Mountainous in the north where it links to the Himalayas, the country narrows to the south and can be described as consisting almost entirely of a river valley. The Irrawaddy river, which I had better call the Ayeyarwady since the government changed its name at the same time as that of the country and various towns, runs for more than 2000 miles from the mountains in the North to the lush delta lands in the South where it discharges into the Andaman Sea. The built up silt of the delta harbours some ten million acres of rice growing and makes Burma a minor food exporter, especially to India, though in economic terms the quantities are pathetic and any major potential revenue earning opportunity is largely stillborn. It is said that the country and the river are one. The Burmese call it a "kind river", because it brings life and it remains largely unpolluted as no factories populate its banks. It is a powerful river too, changing with the seasons, and in places swelling by four times in width and becoming up to 4 miles across in the wet season. In the nineteenth century traditional dispatch boats, powered by forty rowers, took ten days to travel from Rangoon to Mandalay against the current, and four days in the opposite direction. In the dry season, with the river low and quieter, the journey time reduced in both directions.

First impressions were good. The city of Yangon, as the capital Rangoon is now known, is only a short flight from Bangkok. Incidentally did anyone in the government give a thought to how many additional keystrokes all this name changing would make people have to make to write about their country and explain these changes? Imagine if it was suddenly decided to change the name of England to something like Cameronland; and don't think the thought has not crossed his mind – *and by the way Oxford is now Samford*. It could happen, whoever is in power. Another town, Bagan, doubtless also newly named, was set half way to Mandalay and both it and Mandalay were on the river. So a visit to Mandalay could surely be made along the river. I have something of a distaste for large boats and rough seas, or rather my stomach does, but then so did Admiral Nelson, who was evidently a martyr to sea-sickness and still managed to win a few great naval battles. However, pictures of the river all showed it looking sufficiently like the proverbial millpond to calm the fears in even my stomach. So maybe a plan was taking shape.

Unusually the guidebook started with a negative: it made reference to the dismal reputation of the Burmese Government – junta is a better word - with regard to human rights. It actually posed the question as to whether making a visit to the country might endorse or actively help support this oppressive regime and should thus be avoided, though it quickly moved on, saying that, "informed travellers must make up their own minds". Not many guide books try to talk you out of visiting the place they have chosen to describe; though, now I think of it, perhaps something similar could be added to those written about a few other places – *Skip the rest of the book; go somewhere else.*

Burma's military government dates back to 1962, ever since when it has ruled with little popular support, and amid increasing unrest an opposition to the government was set up and the smiling face of its female leader Aung San Suu Kyi quickly became known around the world. 1988 saw a bloody, but ineffectual, series of protests. It took place on 8th of August and "8888" has passed into the language as a mantra of dissatisfaction with the government and an expression of people's desire for freedom and change. Aung San Suu Kyi's NLD party (the National League for Democracy) won a convincing victory in an election, convincing to everyone that is except the ruling party who simply ignored the results and continued to rule. They have kept Aung San Suu Kyi under house arrest for much of the ensuing years. This is no place for an extensive history lesson. Suffice to say that the situation has never been resolved: the government is repressive to the point of using slave labour to work on their chosen projects, some of which, like clearing land for a golf course, are linked to tourism. It spends nearly half of its total budget on its military despite the fact that 60% of the population lives in poverty, and allows one in ten babies to die before their fifth birthday because of the nation's dismal healthcare. It imprisons anyone expressing dissent about government policies and imposes rigorous and widespread censorship.

A special state department called the PRSD (The Press Registration and Scrutiny Department) exists to handle censorship. It checks every single piece of published writing they can get their hands on, from school textbooks to newspapers and magazines. It is common to see magazines sold with pages cut out. There are obvious no-nos; you will not see the word democracy appearing anywhere for instance, but rules are vague and a variety of other topics can find disfavour and prompt the word *hpyoke* (remove) for little apparent reason. Some things are temporary. If the government falls out with a neighbouring state, all mention of that country, its people and anything about it will temporarily disappear. The army of people needed to carry out this task may be good for employment figures and scissors manufacturers, but it does not help inform the Burmese people's view of the world. Publishers can be closed down for long enough to ruin them, so the official line is usually carefully observed. Even so, ways may be found to circumvent officialdom, and it is said that people read carefully between the lines of any apparently innocuous story about animals as allegory may be used to change the government into a snake or an elephant to make a point. What the official scrutinisers would make of any attempt to take the press in a western direction in other ways, with celebrities, gossip, scandal, topless models and advice to stimulate readers' love lives, I really don't know, but no doubt their busy scissors would go into feverish overdrive. Censorship goes further than this however, with what is taught in schools and universities projecting the party line and even those starring in local movies being courted (or bribed or forced?) to support the powers that be. A massive refugee problem exists along the stretch of Thai border located North of Chaing Mai and yet international condemnation of all this seems pretty lacklustre. Even the United States, which seems apt to launch a full-scale invasion of almost anywhere with a government of which it disapproves even slightly, seems inclined to take little action. Thus a beautiful country and its people exist in a kind of limbo with most people hoping for change but keeping their heads down, and an element of civil war rumbling on, especially in the south, while the world does little or nothing about their plight.

Some of this was quite scary. Just the place for a holiday then, I thought.

When making my previous first class journey I had chosen where to go carefully and I had specifically ruled out anywhere with even a hint of danger or unpleasantness about it. I ruled out everywhere involving anything untoward from war zones to man-eating animals; also poisonous insects, a high crime rate or even slightly difficult weather or being located at oxygen starved altitude. In fact I had been so concerned to pick somewhere secure and straightforward that I had even ruled out places with comparatively low level hazards. Australia fell by the wayside as much on the need for British visitors to get a visa as for its proliferation of poisonous spiders. Demanding I got a visa seemed criminal.

Well, there was a time when the population of Australia was mostly made up of deported British convicts and now they want us to ... enough.

My choice then had largely met all these criteria, and certainly the luxury train journey I had made between Singapore and Bangkok was about as unthreatening as travel gets. This kept coming to mind as I contemplated my new trip. Burma sounded wonderful in so many ways, and it was clear that tourists could and did go there, but this coin definitely had two sides to it and if one of them was, well, polished, the other certainly was not. Was I right to go on thinking about it? And if I did go would I be safe?

Burma seemed to me to be a place just somewhat off the beaten track; certainly it was off mine. If living there was a problem for much of its population, then I wanted to be reassured that going there was in no sense a real problem for me. Having picked a country I knew little about and begun to find out about it, it seemed only prudent to check it out further. So, I went on-line. As you do these days. I logged onto the British Foreign Office site that gives advice to travellers and looked up Burma. Oh dear. Ohhhh dear; my plan virtually went on hold there and then. On page one, the very first words were, *You should exercise caution on visits to Burma...*

I won't quote it all, but the following extracts give a flavour:

> *There have been a number of bomb explosions... targets have included places tourists may visit...*
>
> *The political situation in Burma remains unsettled...*
>
> *Typhoons occur in Burma...*
>
> *Credit cards and travellers' cheques are unlikely to be accepted...*

Muggings, burglaries and petty theft in Rangoon have increased... take care of your belongings

Instances of violent crime...

Disruption and restrictions to travel...

Overland travel can be hazardous...

Railway equipment is decrepit...

All British Embassy staff have instructions not to fly with Myanmar Airways...

Health: intrusive medical examinations and emergency dental work should be avoided

It is a malaria area...

In addition, photographing anything military was clearly not a good idea and furthermore, if you did get into any trouble, there was a note explaining that assistance from the British Embassy was not as speedy as in other locations. Given the overall feel of the report I was surprised that there were any British officials in the country at all. To enter this den of uncertainty you had to apply for a visa, which cost £14. Not only were you likely to have problems, you had to pay for the privilege. Various inoculations, and a course of malaria tablets, would add still more to the cost and hassle. Oh dear again.

Given this information off the page, I telephoned hoping for some sort of reassurance. The Foreign Office is a major department of state, and in these days of terrorism, a not unimportant one. I dialled the number on the home page of their travel advice site and, explaining that I was to be writing something about travelling to Burma, asked to speak to someone concerned with their advice page. I was given the number of the main switchboard. Contacting that number I was politely told to phone the first number again and ask to speak to a supervisor. I did that, and the supervisor helpfully explained that I could only access the person to whom I should speak through the main switchboard. I dialled again. Twenty minutes had soon gone by while I did all this; just as well I wasn't trying to report a suspect package outside the British Embassy in Paris, the bomb would have gone off long before I was put through to anyone halfway appropriate.

Eventually I found myself talking to someone actually responsible for the listing of information. More than 300,000 members of the public access the posted advice every month, they told me. There are lots of safety conscious travellers around then; or perhaps some of them are simply armchair travellers providing themselves with an excuse not to go anywhere. Most of the information displayed on the site – 90 per cent of it in fact - originates in the country in question, so in this case there must be a few people in the British Embassy in Rangoon, sorry Yangon. What is posted is reviewed every three months they said, but significant changes and additions are listed as they occur, so it is perfectly possible that some details can change three times in a day. This meant that a particular entry might go perhaps from saying – *What a lovely place,* to *Have a care,* to *Expect to be shipped out in a box* all within the hour. Factual information is the order of the day. If something like a train crash occurs the essential facts of the matter will be posted within minutes. But all the information is strictly objective and non-political. I was told this with great assurance, as if it was a wholly good thing. Yet it meant that the complex and difficult Burmese political situation was described, in a word, as "unsettled". This seemed a little like describing climbing Everest as a bit tricky. As I had already discovered, the only people with a human rights reputation worse than the Burmese government is allegedly Britain's budget airline Ryanair, I wondered if expressing a tad more of an opinion about its nature might actually be helpful. I certainly found it impossible to discover anything in the nature of an opinion during my telephone conversation. If they thought so, why would no one actually say, "This is a right hell hole; you should keep away or being brought home in a box will be the least of your problems"? But the party line expressed on the web site page was departed from by hardly a syllable. Then, right at the end, I did persuade the lady to whom I was talking to say, "strictly off the record", that if she had the opportunity to travel to Burma, then she would do so. Phew, that's alright then.

Not only did it seem that this was a place where some care was necessary, it must be one of the few places in the world that has an organisation engaged in active ongoing lobbying designed to persuade people *not* to go there. Now this may be an odd idea, and one too it occurs to me that could be appropriate for a number of other places ranging from Chelmsford town centre late on a Saturday night to whole countries. That said, and there being such an organisation, I felt I should check it out. I telephoned their offices and arranged to meet someone there, wondering as I did so if my visit might give me irresistible reasons to avoid all the apparent dangers that a trip to Burma evidently entailed.

So, a few days later I found myself at London's Old Street roundabout, surely one of the city's least attractive junctions with its massive advertising signs and soaring steelwork, which is apparently designed to look modern and attractive but just represents a waste of public money. I was there en route to the offices of The Burma Campaign U.K., which describes its remit as to "campaign for human rights and democracy in Burma". Their literature boasts an impressive role call of patrons, an eclectic mix of people including Lord Steel, Maureen Lipman and John Mortimer, and their offices are in a small office building on the corner of a residential square just off the junction. I steeled myself for a walk through the subterranean tunnels beneath the junction and got myself to their front door.

I was greeted by Mark Farmaner, who heads up the organisation, and his assistant, a charming young Burmese woman, who having fled Burma was waiting for the results of her application for political asylum in Britain. She had already been waiting several years with no sign of a resolution. Just a few minutes with these two was enough to convince me of the dastardly nature of the political regime in Burma. The organisation not only raises funds to promote its cause, and campaigns to increase the worldwide political pressure put on the government to change its ways, but they also catalogue the abuse of human rights that is a regular part of life in Burma. Their publications, for example a booklet titled *Eight seconds of silence* about the imprisonment, torture and death of political prisoners that had a long series of mini-biographies of people so treated, make sobering reading. They do not do their work entirely at a distance, but have people making regular visits to the country and to the refugee camps along the Thai border, the "brown areas" where tourists are not permitted. This is a no doubt a risky business for people so outspoken about the regime. Promoting the thought that people should not travel to the country as tourists, as this helps fund the regime and thus contributes to its remaining in power, is only a small part of their brief.

The contrary view is that, for such a closed society, any contact with the outside world provides succour to the people and financial help too, because some of the money someone spends on a visit goes directly to individuals or helps them remain in employment in hotels and other establishments directly relating to catering for international visitors. The negative campaign certainly has some effect. For example, certain tour companies make a point of not offering Burma as a destination. Still people do go. The figures seemed difficult to validate, but something between 400 and 700 thousand people visit Burma every year. This is small beer compared with other countries in the region: Singapore has three or four times its own population visiting it in a year. But it is still a significant number.

Mark was certainly passionate in his belief about this, and I could see the sense of it in some ways, but two things weighed on the scales in making a personal judgement: first, while visiting would inevitably give some money to the government, it would give money to others too and that could, in a small way, perhaps help. Secondly, as I planned to write about my visit if I made one, I felt that I should judge it personally and in situ and reserve judgement on whether I would come down on one side or the other of the argument until I had seen something of the place for myself.

I thanked Mark, departed with a pile of literature and promised to let him know what I did and how I got on.

Even with all the negative information I had collected, and despite my instinct for self-preservation and a comfortable life, the place just became more and more fascinating as I read more about it. I wanted to go and see it, even if I ended up recommending that others did not follow in my footsteps. With my plan intact, I had to finance and configure the trip. Unfortunately, I had no reserves of air miles to cover the flights. I have always been jealous of David Phillips, an American who found that he could collect 500 air miles against bar codes for a frozen pudding product in a promotion. He also discovered that he could buy individual servings in packs of ten, each with its own bar code, for 25 cents. He scoured stores and accumulated more than 12,000 packs. Having done this he had no time to take off the labels before the offer closed, so he donated the food to a charity on condition that they took off the labels and returned them to him. He submitted his entry and received 1,253,000 miles of free air travel, which, being more than a million, gave him gold status and even more benefits. For a modest outlay he had virtually a lifetime of free flights.

My friend Silvia uses a lovely phrase and talks about what she describes as "mad money". This describes money set aside to finance indulgences, things that are strictly unnecessary, but which also constitute unmissable treats. Such things include chocolate, shoes and more. As I intended to travel in style, my planned trip would need not so much mad money as totally insane money. But, whatever the cost, there must surely be ways of doing it that minimised the hazards and thus my fears. Nothing ventured, nothing gained, I thought. Visiting Burma may not be all be plain sailing but let's assume that, on balance, it is worthwhile. I remembered what

Dorothy had said when she returned from the Land of Oz, "Some of it wasn't very nice, but most of it was beautiful". Right. I would fix myself a beautiful, first-class trip, perhaps it would be better described as fearfully first class.

Chapter Two

WAY TO GO

*"An agreeable companion on a journey
is as good as a carriage."*
Publius Syrus

With Mandalay as my chosen destination, the next job was to make the necessary arrangements. Burma borders Bangladesh, China, Thailand and Laos. It is a large country, one as geographically large as the United Kingdom and France combined, its people are divided into eight main groups: the Burman, Shan, Mon (the group who first introduced Buddhism to Burma), Rakhaing, Kayin, Kayah, Chin and Kachin. These are said in turn to sub-divide into nearly a hundred ethnic sub groups. They add up to a population of over 50 million people. Those opposed to the government call them "fifty million hostages". It is also tied to the rest of the world, well let's say loosely, with most of its attention focused inwards and a good deal of it on stopping or limiting contacts with other countries, other than those few, like China, that give significant economic support. Unsurprisingly perhaps, you cannot fly direct from London to Mandalay. I actually found this fact rather reassuring: having decided to travel to somewhere that was not yet firmly on the mass tourism map, it would have been too simple to have just boarded a flight and disembarked in the city itself; anyone could do that. Besides, having consulted various guidebooks and maps, I had formed a vision in my mind of arriving in Mandalay by travelling along the splendid-looking Ayerdarwady River. The most logical route seemed to be to fly to Yangon via Bangkok and make my way from there. No problem: Bangkok is a place I know and a city that would make a worthy starting point.

I continued my research and visited a couple of travel agents. Do I love travel agents or hate them? For the most part let's go with hate. I tend to view them as being rather like estate agents: believing that actually no one really likes them, but that we grudgingly admit that they do have a certain use if you go travelling. The first job is to get to talk to someone. Usually when you go in every agent is busy; they acknowledge your presence in no way whatsoever and all seem intent on conversations that look set to last until closing time. If you feel rejected when your analyst fails to return your call, then this will convince you of your utter invisibility. People do move on eventually though, or they do so once they have sufficient information to go home and book something on the Internet, so let's assume you get to speak to someone. My mother always said that the worst thing you can say about anyone is that they "mean well". And this is surely an appropriate comment here. I'm sure travel agents do mean well, but they rarely seem to have any immediate knowledge of anything you ask them about and spend what seems like forever doing the modern equivalent of looking vexed and sucking their pencils, by looking vexed and poring over a computer. They normally do this with the computer screen firmly facing towards them and with little or no commentary, so, with no more than the occasional mouse clicks to guide you, you never know how close you are getting to a solution. These deliberations tend to be punctuated by the person doing them pausing to answer the telephone or deciding that, given the rarefied nature of your enquiry, they had better hand over to Deirdre or whoever as, "I only started here yesterday and, like basically, I don't know the system." When Deirdre appears she is likely to be no better informed. Indeed most of those working in high street travel agencies seem so young that they have surely hardly had time to travel from the last day at school to the first day at work, much less to garner any experience of the world. Whoever you deal with, it's rather like unerringly getting in the slowest queue at an airport. In this case you always seem to spend twenty minutes getting nowhere, though the person next to you seems somehow to be getting just what they want. Other customers always seem to be at the stage of considering the minutiae of the arrangements they are making – *If I have a room on the third floor rather than the fourth will I be nearer the ice-making machine, further from the elevator and still have a balcony?* The details are important certainly, but sitting next to this sort of thing waiting for an initial response to my enquiry just makes me despair of ever getting that far. Another hazard is that if you ask for a holiday in Spain or a villa in Tuscany, say, then you quickly discover the fact that such present about a gazillion differing options and this compounds these problems further. This time, however, I had a simple question, one that produced few options: Burma? Mandalay? In style. How? In due time I left clutching a manageable number of brochures.

I wondered if, in the interests of comprehensiveness, I might also usefully embrace modern technology and consult the Internet, but Burma was not as yet in my favourites file and Googling it produced a list of *about* 29,000,000 references. *About?* Even the mighty Google did not seem sure in how many places I needed to look. I examined the brochures and they seemed up to the job, and certainly amongst comparatively few options that met my planned journey objectives one stood out. One was head and shoulders above the others. You could indeed visit Mandalay arriving from the river; indeed you could apparently do it in real style on the aptly named river cruiser, *Road to Mandalay*. This was not just any old boat either, it was the flagship as it were of a travel operator specialising in the first class end of the market and operating a chain of tempting looking hotels, and a variety of journeys including the famous Orient Express trains. It looked good in the pictures, as it sailed serenely on a calm river with sunset lit pagodas in the background, and by comparison it seemed any other river transport was best described as a rust bucket. It seemed as if this way of doing things might put some of my still lingering fears to rest.

But given my distaste for ships, could I trust myself to such a vessel? I checked the details. The cruiser is just over one hundred meters long, and twelve-and–a-half metres wide. It has a draft of less than one-and-a-half-meters. There are 58 cabins and when full she can carry 110 passengers. The specific brochure about it lacks nothing in confidence, saying: *All the cabins are carefully designed with handpicked fabrics, and equipped with en-suite bathrooms and air conditioning. On deck there is a swimming pool and comfortable, shaded seating, providing the ideal setting to savour the peaceful serenity of the Ayeyarwady and its people.* The journey was described as one of ... *genuine distinction, of rare authenticity...*

it was... *triumphant proof that the golden age of travel lives on.* It added, by way of summary, that: *A journey along this mighty river is a voyage of a lifetime* and that all this should appeal to *discerning travellers with a sense of adventure.* There was apparently no need to dwell on safety. The brochure said simply that the cruiser... *meets all international safety requirements for river vessels of her classification;* it did not mention life rafts once. I could have done with reading all this as I sat next to Harold on my ill-fated Singapore flight. Perhaps a selection of upmarket travel brochures should always go in your hand luggage when you fly economy, though with security as it is these days the airline might well confiscate them in case they upset the other passengers. This sounded very much to be the way to fulfil my newfound ambition of seeing Mandalay in some style.

Reading more about the cruiser, I discovered that it had been built in 1964 and ... now wait just a minute: 1964 is a l-o-n-g time ago. 1964! Was this thing still watertight? Suddenly I was not sure whether this was very appealing prospect after all. I would not want to fly in a 40+ year-old airliner: it would probably be a biplane with its wings joined together with string, rattling propellers and an outside toilet. There were already sufficient potential hazards going round in my mind, and I felt this unexpected fact stood some more investigation.

I discovered that the *Road to Mandalay* was built as the *Nederland* in Cologne, Germany to cruise on the river Rhine. In 1964 she was a classy piece of work and plied her trade successfully until vessels with shallower drafts, able to access larger tracts of the river, took her place. She was then renamed *Elbresidenz* and moved 200 miles to the river Elbe where she acted as a floating hotel. In 1994 she was purchased and underwent a US$ 6 million refit in Hamburg designed to turn her into the pride of the Ayerdarwady. Now practically a new boat she was all ready for her new role. There was one snag: the Ayerdarwady is more than 5000 miles away from Germany. So she was loaded onto a specialist transport ship, the *Condock IV*, a process that involved sinking the transport to a depth at which the *Road to Mandalay* could be floated on, then pumping the ballast tanks dry so that the transport floated up carrying her charge with her. This all sounded pretty clever and it was presumably done with some confidence, though personally I would have been a tad suspicious of a ship with the number IV after her name. Whatever happened to the first three? Maybe they too were filled with water to take on some heavy cargo and never came back up. Be that as it may, *Condock IV* set sail on 31 August 1995 travelling down the English Channel, through the Suez Canal and on to Rangoon as it was then, where *Road to Mandalay* was successfully unloaded and sailed up the Ayerdarwady ready to go about her new duties. Her final fitting and decoration was completed in Burma, so that the style, fabrics, colours and local antiques created an authentic and pleasing atmosphere and, rather like the ugly duckling become a swan, she set off on her first journey on her new river in December 1995.

Life is so unpredictable. One minute you are floating happily on the Elbe with nothing much to worry about and every prospect of seeing out your life in quiet tranquillity, and the next you find yourself literally being torn apart and apparently reduced to scrap. Then, far from being used as raw material to build containers or something, you find yourself being put back together again, and shipped half way across the world. Never mind, after a long journey you find you have been given a whole new river to play with and also that you have to suffer no more winters freezing your Plimsoll line.

On learning all this, I decided that if I regarded the ship as effectively starting life in 1995, then that was hardly more than ten years back. On that basis she should still be in good nick and besides I also discovered that she had no fewer than four engines. I wondered why exactly – did they not expect more than three of them to break down on a voyage or was there one for each direction? In any case I found such a number strangely comforting.

Yes, this was just the job. This was all I needed to fulfil my ambition. First I needed to turn some savings into mad money - well, mad, mad, mad money. Then all I needed to do was to clear a space in my diary, make a reservation, apply for and get a visa, fix flights, organise various vaccinations and a supply of anti-malaria pills, book somewhere to stay in Bangkok, pack a suitcase and remember to switch on the answering machine before leaving the house.

There was conflicting advice about the malaria situation. The boat's operator's said not only that it was not necessary to take precautions, but also that few passengers taking the trip did so. However, various guides and web sites labelled Burma as firmly and irrevocably in an area of high risk. To be sure, I booked an appointment with my GP, or rather with the practice Travel Nurse. Doing so took time of course, with my suggestion of Thursday being replaced with suggestions of the following month and queries about which year we were talking about. But it seemed better to postpone the trip than make it earlier and come back to a lifetime of recurrent fevers. Maybe lots of people were off to exotic places at the time or the nurse was unavailable for a while because she was travelling herself. Once I was sitting in front of her, she consulted her travel bible, confirmed the necessity to take precautions, wrote me a prescription for anti-malaria pills and whacked into me a vaccination concoction through what seemed to me to be an industrial-sized syringe for good measure. Ouch! I still wondered if it was all necessary, but wondered too what Britain's great National Health Service would say if I failed to take the recommended precautions and then came back with the disease asking for help. "You were warned, nothing we can do now, budgets being what they are. You certainly can't have a bed, but we might be able to let you die in a corridor, if you are quick about it." Anyway it was done and one potential hazard could be ticked off as dealt with.

My mind still dwelt on other hazards. One hazard was snakes, which are not my favourite thing. They seemed to love Burma, which had more than one hundred and fifty species, thirty-seven of them poisonous. Some sources suggested that species such as Russell's vipers, kraits and king cobras awaited you every few yards. In the waiting room at the doctor's surgery just prior to my appointment, I had seen a list as I scanned through an old magazine. The item was headed: "Top 10 Heaviest animals". It helpfully listed everything from insects – the 12 centimetre long Goliath beetle, a native of Africa, can evidently grow to weigh 100 grams - to dinosaurs – the sauropod Bruhathkayosuarus was the world's largest weighing up to 240,000 kg - though you are unlikely to bump into the first unless you visit Africa and the second would make more than a bump, but is of course extinct. Heading number six was "living snakes": the largest, which took nine people to lift its 182.76 kg, was a Burmese python. Never mind mosquitoes, I wondered if I could be inoculated against meeting even its younger brother. Burma had poisonous spiders too, and earthquakes, typhoons and ... but I was determined not to get scared about any such thing.

Next I turned to the travel arrangements: I booked flights, and here I do not just mean a flight out and a flight back, I mean flights. Perhaps I may digress for a moment, because thanks are due to the many people who read *First class at last* and wrote to me saying something like, "Didn't your wife travel with you?" Well, no (the trip was work, after all), but your comments helped make very sure she did this time. Another solo work trip to somewhere so enticing was clearly not on; realistically some things do have a certain inevitability about them. If I'm honest I do enjoy travelling alone, but also on occasion I was happy to subscribe to the view that solitude is only a good idea if you have the right people with you to share it.

Because I have been self-employed for many years and because my business has regularly taken me overseas, especially to South East Asia, I have got into the habit of making travel arrangements on an independent basis in order to produce the necessary flexibility. I maintained this habit. I booked flights with a travel agent recommended by Thai Airways. When my budget really matters they come up with good prices and make it worth seeking them out even though they are hardly accessible, being on the far side of London from where I live. Recently I have been able to circumvent their labrynthine telephone procedure, which starts by asking what language you want to conduct business in, something that makes me want to press the *No jargon, ambiguities or hold ups* button, by finding someone who I can email. I set out details, get a quote back by email and then they telephone me to make the booking. So this was done promptly.

I had already booked the river trip itself together with the linking flights from Bangkok to Yangon and on to Bagan where the river journey began (sic) liaising directly with the ship's operator. As befits so prestigious a company this was an entirely hassle-free process and the tickets and other details arrived in a classy portfolio that made my current briefcase seem tatty. Was there anything else? Visas were necessary and getting visas can be a problem for many countries; not least embassies seem to want to hold onto your passport for long periods of time, which you then have to ensure do not clash with a need to travel anywhere else. In this case a telephone call had the necessary forms arriving the following day. They were simple to complete and having sent them off with our passports, and the ubiquitous appalling photographs, they duly arrived back within 48 hours; an indication of the small number of visas that they issue perhaps.

Right, check: what else? Insurance: covered on an annual policy. A hotel in Bangkok: booked direct with an email. A taxi to the airport: booked for some unearthly hour on the morning of departure because the route from my home to London's Heathrow airport is along the infamous ring road: the M25. If you live in the U.K. then nothing else needs to be said. If not, think of six lanes of packed traffic moving slowly along a main road and regularly passing accidents and road works that slow things up still more.

Everything seemed set. Provided we spent the next three weeks considering and doing our packing, my wife assured me that everything was in hand. I got the suitcases out of the cupboard to her schedule, saw again the dent in my somewhat battered one and thought of something said by Yogi Berra: "Why buy good luggage? You only use it when you travel." Perhaps a dented suitcase should be regarded as a badge of honour in the battle to travel and survive.

Chapter Two

Chapter Three

A GOOD START

"There is no moment of delight in any pilgrimage like the beginning of it."
Charles Dudley Wilson

Some people don't like flying, some are frightened of it, and most would agree that it would be a whole lot better if you were able to step straight from your living room into the plane. But of course you can't do that. However, on this occasion the preliminaries went well. The alarm went off at the right time, my suitcase closed without an unholy fight to get it shut and the need to get my taxi driver to sit on it, and the journey to London's Heathrow was no more horrendous or lengthy than expected. What can one say about Heathrow? The *Daily Telegraph* described it recently as "the most depressing word in the English language". The horrors this national embarrassment inflicts on hapless travellers would fill a whole book, and perhaps one could put alongside it the fact that British Airways has recently been announced as top of a European airline league table: it loses more luggage than any other airline. Not my problem this time, at least. I was heading East and this time I found that the Thai Airways check–in area was not crowded; well actually it was very crowded for economy but, on this occasion of course, I swept past that and had my boarding pass within moments. I was on my own, acting as scout for the expedition as it were, set to attend to some business first and then join up with my wife as she arrived in Bangkok for our flight onwards to Yangon in five or six days time. She had almost an extra week to finish her packing, something that was proving slightly vexing as on the internal flights in Burma small aircraft meant a lower than usual weight allowance for luggage. Despite this I got a message during that week saying she had found an irresistible and unrepeatable deal and, "can I buy a new suitcase?" I just knew it would be larger than her current one. Still, naturally keen to do anything I could to help reduce her packing nightmare, I agreed uncomplainingly. I claim to be able to pack in about fifteen minutes, but having said that, I must admit that this is only because everything is ironed and ready for me when I do. This time when she came to do hers, that kitchen sink would just have to stay at home.

It took a lot of the hassle out of the overall process to spend the waiting time until the flight in the executive lounge, board the plane ahead of the rush and turn left towards the front of the plane on boarding to find my seat in the upstairs cabin. Despite this plain sailing there is always something. This time the man in front of me going through security waited until he was at the front of the queue before doing any of the things that are now necessary to go further. He must have been going to a cold country, because he carefully took off three layers of coats and jackets, took long minutes to retrieve his laptop computer and various leads and plugs from the bowels of his enormous flight bag, and then instigated a full scale search by making the X-ray machine buzz like an angry wasp when he went through with a ton of small change distributed around several pockets. He dropped them all as he got them out. Eventually I was able to follow him through, and stood waiting while he stood in a sea of small change to have his bag opened and searched leaving mine stuck further back, and then left him scrabbling on the floor so that he could redistribute what looked like coins from six different currencies in the various pockets of his many jackets.

My flight was uneventful; perhaps a word to hope will apply to every flight you ever take. It was due to arrive early in the morning. So I only had two or three hours before it was time to settle down to sleep if I wanted to have eight hours rest and wake up as we landed as part of my habitual attempt to minimise the effects of jet lag and get onto the right time at my destination. I followed my normal routine: duly swallowed a sleeping pill, put in my ear plugs and, having told the flight attendant not to wake me for anything, especially an emergency, I pulled down my eye mask and settled down. I slumbered away the miles in a comfortable seat placed well out of reach of twitching elbows. I woke only as the landing announcement boomed out.

The plane had arrived on time and duly landed at Bangkok's new airport: Suvarnabhumi. It perhaps illustrates the controversy surrounding this project to say that questions have been asked about it in the Houses of Parliament: the British one that is, where MPs have expressed concern and asked for assurances that it is safe for British travellers to fly into it. A project designed to give Thailand the flagship airport of South East Asia and boost their business as a stopover and transfer point for flights onwards to Australia and other places around Asia Pacific, has instead produced criticism, chaos and costs way beyond the initial estimates. So much so that, as I write this, Don Muang, the old airport, is being reopened and a proportion of domestic flights are being moved back to there to try to help sort out the problems.

It is certainly a puzzle. Superficially it looks to be an iconic modern design. Steel arches reminiscent of the Sydney Opera House tower one on another and much of it looks and is good. But the design seems odd to say the least. There is air-conditioning that fails to reduce the humid temperature in some areas, and there are many curious bottlenecks around the terminal; there just does not seem to be space where space is needed. Check-in lines stretch back so that they meet in the centre of the space designed for them, which is an area supposed to accommodate people walking through. Various corridors and aisles are so narrow that it is difficult for two passengers pushing trolleys in different directions to pass each other let alone more. In other areas the lighting is so dim you expect Alien to jump out into the steel corridors and devour you. In addition this is the only place in the whole world, and ever in my entire life, where I have had to queue for the loo. No sympathy from my wife when I told her about *that*. She laughed, and said that if it upset me that much it was lucky I was not a woman. There is one thing for which sufficient space does seem to have been provided, of course, and that is shops. What a surprise. They line the seemingly endless corridors and sell everything you can possibly imagine.

Since it opened for business late in 2006 the newspapers have reported the unfolding drama. Costs have overrun, they say. Controls have been inadequate, corruption has been rife and generally things could have gone better. Thailand's popular King has steadfastly declined to perform any sort of official opening, understandably not wanting to do so with builders still working in the background, I guess. It prompts the old question: conspiracy or cock-up? And the answer seems to be some, actually perhaps quite a bit of both. Worst of all, stretches of runway and taxiway are cracking and sinking – the whole place was built on marshland and was supposed to have been drained to make it secure. Now emergency drainage work is under way to sort the matter out, and it is this that has been causing capacity problems and necessitating some flights to be moved elsewhere. Tortrakul Yomnak, Chief Engineer of Airports of Thailand, is reported as saying, "We can fix it". That's alright then; though much the same was said in UK about the ill-fated Millenium Dome project. Who is ultimately responsible for all this is not yet clear; meanwhile the architects, who are based in Chicago, are saying little that I have seen reported.

Anyway, it was into this miracle of modern technology and economics that I was unloaded. Despite the fact that the airport was built to take traffic up by tens of millions of passengers a year on present levels, despite the *Baht* 155 billion spent on the construction, despite the 120 bays for aircraft to load and unload at, passengers were disgorged into buses. We were then delivered to the furthest corner of the airport building and left to walk what seemed almost as far as we had flown to find our luggage and passport control. I collected my suitcase, on this occasion tagged "Priority", and which was satisfyingly amongst the first dozen to appear, and went to find a taxi to take me to my hotel. My driver was about forty years old, I would estimate, and, unusually for a Thai, almost completely bald. What hair he had was white and so was his designer stubble. He wore a T-shirt extolling the virtues of *Singha* beer and sunglasses better suited to a fighter pilot. Now some people have sunglasses in the form of clip-ons that they attach to their prescription spectacles, but my driver had his set up the other way round, he had clip on prescription glasses clipped to his trendy sunglasses. I commented on this oddity and he laughed. "One to keep out sun, one to let in seeing," he said and promptly flipped the seeing bit up. The first stretch of road from the new airport is itself newly built and the area to either side of it is empty and uninteresting. Work of some sort continues along here; there is a rail link going in, for instance, and there are several encampments of corrugated iron roofed shanties, which house construction workers in something less than luxurious conditions. Stubble man whisked me passed all this, through two toll points and on towards the city. He drove perfectly well without his prescription glasses, but flipped them down again for the last stretch once we were off the toll highway and into traffic.

There had been no hesitation in booking The Oriental Hotel in Bangkok as somewhere to stay for a few nights en route to and from Burma. I had stayed there on my previous journey, but my wife had never stayed there. However, her knowledge of its reputation, and experience of having dinner there on previous visits to the city (twice now I think about it - I must watch these absurd fits of generosity) had made an impression on her that could not be swayed. Besides, it is an exceptional hotel.

Just arriving in the lobby sets the scene. It is a dramatic space, opulent, and dominated by large bell-like lights, yet still conveying an intimacy that is reinforced by the immediate and welcoming service that is received by every visitor. I once watched the same seat sat in by three different people one after the other. Each spent just a minute sitting there rising almost at once to meet someone and heading off elsewhere. Each time in the brief gap, a member of staff went and plumped up the cushion. Not even the tiniest variation from the pristine is permitted to spoil the effect for even a moment.

I checked in painlessly. There can be exceptions to this, however. On my last visit to Singapore I checked into a hotel and pointed out to them that I was booked for three nights not four as it said on the registration form given to me to sign. The receptionist looked confused. "But we have you down for four nights," he said. "You may well have, but it's three," I replied. "I don't think we can change that," he said. Not change it? What? What exactly did he mean? Was I to be locked in my room so that I was physically unable to depart? I know you can be fined for a long list of misdemeanours in Singapore, but surely not incarcerated for *under* staying at a hotel. He hesitated, but agreed I would not be imprisoned, adding for the third time, "I am sure you stay here for four." We agreed to differ and I went to my room. When I departed as planned there was no comment. Before I left I had told a friend of mine I was to stay at the Oriental and, although she had never stayed there herself, she told me that she had once arranged and paid for a three night stay at the hotel for her daughter. She was arriving in Bangkok at the end of a gap year break spent travelling around the region. When she arrived at the door she looked so dirty and dishevelled after three months on the road that she was refused entry. The doorman gave her a "we can't have scruffs like you cluttering up the lobby, lowering the tone and frightening our respectable guests" speech, though I am sure he put it very diplomatically. Just saying she was expected and wanted to check in was not enough. The doorman insisted on phoning through to reception to verify that she had a reservation. She must have been seriously scruffy; I hope she spoke to her welcomer again once she had spent a transforming time in her smart bathroom.

Even after a long journey, I was evidently smart enough to avoid such as this and soon found myself in a wonderful room on the fifth floor with a spectacular view across Bangkok's busy Chao Phya River. I unpacked hastily, forgoing the services of the room's butler who offered to help, and headed off to the Terrace for a late breakfast. Sleeping soundly on the plane beneath my "do not disturb" sign had meant no breakfast on board at whatever unearthly hour they had served it. The plane had landed on time and I had got into the city promptly. It was now still only a little after nine a.m. and breakfast here promised to be a much more civilized affair than a tray on the plane, even if it had not been an economy one I had missed. So it proved.

After a few days of business I was back at The Oriental ready for my wife's arrival the following morning. Even for a day or two being here was a real luxury, an experience to savour, though I discovered that for some people it was a way of life. Collecting some cereal to start my buffet breakfast, I found myself standing on the terrace alongside the river. An American, who, from his appearance, might have been an accountant or a lawyer, was feeding the fish that congregate in the water below. Some were fully four foot long, a testament to the nutritious nature of the Oriental's bread – even yesterday's crusts, which the management brought out in a bag for this purpose. We exchanged a brief word and I asked how long he was staying for. "Just through February and March," he said, as if a couple of months in one of the world's best hotels was a mere routine weekend break. I did not know whether to be pleased for him or upset that I could not do the same. No matter: my stay here was short but there was a new adventure to come on the river. I returned to my breakfast. My tea was refilled on numerous occasions at just the right moments. The fruit was delectable, the eggs perfectly cooked and the pastries and breads, successfully tested by the fish, were a temptation not to be wholly resisted. I could have sat there a long time.

I did.

Breakfast is only part of what this great hotel has to offer, of course. It has a number of excellent restaurants, a bar in which top-notch jazz singers perform, and all the facilities you would expect of such an exalted property. But if you twist my arm and ask me to name just one thing that makes it special, then it has to be the staff. The service is wholly excellent, of course, but this coupled with the smiles, charm and grace of the Thais makes it truly exceptional. Even the most routine request is responded to without fail in a delightful manner, and anything out of the ordinary is treated as a challenge to be delivered in style. Later in our stay as we went from the room to the elevator, my wife asked the butler on our floor if he knew about a football match she hoped to get the result of later. He assured her he would check, telling her proudly and in a confidential tone that David Beckham no less had stayed on the floor below only a few months ago. He had not met him, but he had seen him in the flesh and that's not something that happens in just any old hotel. He was clearly a fan. When we returned to the room after dinner, he greeted us with an enigmatic smile, led the way to our room, opened the door for us and revealed the television already turned on and showing the match concerned on some obscure satellite channel. Excellent; her team won too.

The bedroom was comfortable, well equipped and quiet. It was air conditioned as you would expect in such a hot country, but had the quietest air-con I think I have ever come across. Most people find air-conditioning essential in this part of the world, and indeed it does get very hot; and sometimes very, *very* hot. So hot in fact that in the 1500s as the world was still being explored there was a time when people believed that at the equator the sea boiled. They must have thought that preparing an instant fish dish was easy. At worst in lesser hotels the air-con alone, groaning and rattling through the night can spoil a stay, certainly a night's sleep. Other things too can disturb your night in a hotel. In one hotel room I had on a Singapore visit I made the mistake of accepting a room with a connecting door linking through to the next door room. At 2 a.m. my neighbour's television was still so loud that sleep was impossible. I had been putting off doing anything about it (why do we do such things? Fear of reprisal?), but finally phoned Reception, heard the phone ring next door and silence immediately descended. The next morning I met the lady next door. We emerged from our rooms at the same time, and on seeing me she was instantly all apologies. She had gone into her room about ten o'clock after a long journey, put the television on while she unpacked and then lay down on the bed. The next moment she was sound asleep, then the phone was ringing and she was still lying there fully dressed. I could have saved us both some trouble by phoning earlier; I was the only one hearing the television. Ever since then I have resolved never to accept a room with a door like that again.

The following morning, I had set the alarm for 6.30a.m. Two things struck me about this: first I wondered if the floor's indefatigable butler – Wirat was the one who most often seemed to be on duty, though shifts brought both men and women to the role at different times – would deliver me a cup of tea and nudge me gently awake as an alternative to the shock of a raucous alarm. Probably, but the alarm seemed simpler, even if I felt that any sort of early morning alarm was rather at odds with the level of spoilt luxury I was indulging in. Its incessant buzz duly woke me and I immediately called the Business Centre, or whoever handles such things at that time of the morning, and asked them to check if my wife's flight would be landing on time. I had a date for breakfast, but first I had promised to be bright eyed and in the lobby when she arrived. Bearing in mind the splendid hotel, which I had arranged for her to stay in, she had kindly offered to allow me a little longer in bed and to find her own way in from the airport. As I shaved, the phone rang: the flight was on time, I was told politely. It was good to have had someone else battle uncomplainingly through whatever system the airline had to provide this sort of information. I imagined a long series of "please wait" signals and options to key in – *Is the flight today, tomorrow or too far ahead for you to be bothering us with this today?* – and reckoned I was well out of it. I continued with my getting-up-chores and was comfortably ensconced in the lobby in good time for her arrival. Her carefully packed suitcase, its precise contents so long carefully contemplated ahead of the journey, was rapidly sent up to the room. Wirat, who worked from a desk nearby, greeted her warmly as she stepped out of the elevator and escorted us to the room. After taking time for only a quick wash and brush up we were on our way down to breakfast and she was finally able to appreciate the Oriental's special charms first-hand.

The place seemed to live up to her expectations. Phew, thank goodness. It really is very special and deserves the many accolades it receives. Given the long haul flight one of us had just made, we spent a quiet day pottering around the hotel and by the pool enjoying the view across the river, catching up and anticipating the journey that lay ahead. In the evening the hotel hosted a wedding with some 700 guests. We watched for a while in the lobby as people arrived and went up the staircase to the Mezzanine floor. Never have I seen so much silk finery in one place. It was clear that this was to be a grand event.

We ate an early supper and retired in good time; the next day we would move countries.

Chapter Four

A DIFFERENT WORLD

"Stop worrying about the potholes in the road
and enjoy the journey."
Babs Hoffman

Yangon is only an hour away from Bangkok by air. It is, I discovered, an hour that takes you into a very different world. An early flight meant that the day started at 5 a.m. with another trip to Suvarnabhumi airport. Checking in was easier than last time I flew out of the airport as First and Business class passengers now had a completely separate check in area. There were seats at the counters, few people about and our pre-reserved aircraft seating appeared from the system just as it should do. This section also has its own dedicated passport control point and so progress to the lounge was swift. I checked my emails on one of the computers that are now a key part of any airline lounge. As so often, half the machines had dark, blank screens labelled "Out of Order"; one of the staff told me that people steal the mouses (mice?). I only had five messages, but one demanded a reply and necessitated consulting my diary, which took a while as it was buried in my carry-on case.

This done, it was time to go to the gate where people were already climbing onto buses. No pier again. It was a bit of a scrum, but for us, with a bus dedicated to those with seats in the upper classes, at least it was a better class of scrum. We arrived safely at the plane and found the front cabin less than half full. Breakfast arrived shortly after take off, and the flight information screen showed only 58 minutes to go as we tucked into a croissant and the kind of scrambled egg with which you could lag a loft. I recently discovered that one of the reasons that I dislike almost all airline food is that the hypoxic conditions in the cabin, that's the lower than usual oxygen levels, significantly affect your sense of taste. For example, because low oxygen makes hormone levels change, your ability to taste sour and bitter tastes declines and that for sweet tastes is heightened. The net effect is that everything is scrambled and nothing tastes quite like it should; a bit like the egg. So it's not entirely the airline's fault that their culinary skills appear to be barely formed.

Everyone around looked happy, no one appeared to be having any doubts about the wisdom of going to Burma and the steward in charge of our seats spent time giving us a delightful pitch for his furniture business. This was, he said, his young face beaming with entrepreneurial zeal, "just a hobby". That it might have been, but he was still keen to drum up business, praised the quality of what he sold to the skies and drew us a map to indicate where his shop was located on the edge of Bangkok's largest weekend market. We promised to look him up if we visited the market in the future. This was certainly a novelty: you might expect to come off a flight with a couple of magazines picked up from a nearby seat pocket, but not with a table, six chairs and an antique cupboard.

We put our watches back half an hour from Thai time, and observed the countryside below change from cityscape to green fields to beautiful mountains and then to a more arid landscape. In what seemed no time we were on the ground again and off the plane; the steward wished us goodbye with a final "See you at market. My furniture the best" and we were into another bus, this time for the short run to the terminal. Back home we had received dire warnings about passport control and entry into the country; it was evidently slow and bureaucratic, and officials were prone to pounce on anything the least bit untoward. It had been suggested in London that I made sure that my passport did not list my occupation as writer, this being likely to have me shadowed throughout my visit by military intelligence personnel eager to check each and every word I wrote in my notebook. This could have made things difficult. I often have difficulty reading the notes I have scribbled down on a journey, so what anyone else would make of them I do not know, especially someone whose first language was not English – *What means "Furniture steward's pitch"?* However, despite the fact that there were two officials at each check point – one to check up on the other, perhaps - this did not arise and we sailed through immigration without any problem in no time at all. In fact the officials smiled and welcomed us.

The airport was small and a glass wall fronted the luggage hall. I waved through it to a smiling lady in a large white sunhat who was holding up a sign with the name of our hotel on it. Her smile broadened and she waved back. Only a few minutes later, with the suitcases safely retrieved and on a trolley, we went out to meet her. We had to wait for a German couple going to the same hotel, but they were evidently in line not far behind. When they joined us, I asked whether they could speak English, the woman answered with a brief, "No". Once outside we crossed the forecourt, sunlit but just a little cooler and less humid than sweltering Bangkok and everyone piled into a battered mini-van. It was the sort of thing that you see parked in certain streets in London with a "For Sale" notice on it, placed there by young Australian tourists who have driven them all the way from home across the many potholes of every underdeveloped country they passed through on the way. This looked to me to be decidedly less than first class. We were going to a smart hotel and I had naturally expected to be transported in some style. As we made our way out of the bustling airport pick-up area I changed my view: this was veritably the Rolls Royce of local mini-vans. It was soon surrounded by vehicles of all sorts, nearly all of them older looking than ours and most seemingly in dire need of care and attention.

As we pulled onto the road the driver apparently shot straight into the wrong lane. I braced for a collision, though it quickly became apparent that every other driver was doing the same thing. I had been confused by the fact that we were in a right hand drive vehicle, which I had sort of assumed would drive on the left. Not so: the rule of the road was to drive on the right. However, almost all the vehicles were second – or maybe third or fourth – hand. Economics dictated that they were imported from Japan where people drive on the left. It was explained to me later that, despite the rule of the road having been switched from driving on the left to on the right some ten years previously, this mismatch was a long-standing local anomaly. Drivers adjusted and made it work, and presumably people like taxi drivers who spent all day in their cars could be spotted as they walked along the road with their heads permanently bent to the left. Drivers made it work, but it was just a little bit unnerving.

Our smiling, sun-hatted guide had introduced herself as Gi-Gi. Such people must be an amalgam of shepherd, nanny, diplomat and teacher. She proved to combine such characteristics charmingly and efficiently and quickly began to tell us about our schedule. It was a ride of thirty minutes or so to the hotel, and in the afternoon we would have a tour to show us something of Yangon. She told us a little to set the scene. The port city, surrounded on three sides by water, had been inhabited for 2500 years; it was now home to some 4 million people and it was growing fast (its population had quadrupled in thirty years). It had a turbulent history and in more recent years had been captured by the British during the first Anglo-Burmese war in 1824 (there were three such wars), was destroyed by fire in 1849 and, once rebuilt, almost completely destroyed again in the next war. Its most famous landmark was the famous and spectacular ancient Shwedagon Pagoda, which we would visit later.

During this explanation, we proceeded through the traffic with the driver's helper sitting in the left hand seat to act as his eyes on that side and make up for his odd driving position. Any overtaking involved a large degree of consultation but proceeded without a hitch. The noise outside came from the age of the vehicles around us. Rattles and bangs punctuated the roar of elderly engines, and fumes sufficient to make any scientist's most pessimistic estimates about global warming severely understated, rose above the slightly uneven road. I saw a bus with the space beside its driver piled high with cans of diesel, and another with no cover over the engine at the back. A huge flywheel spun unprotected inches from anyone crossing behind it. The roads themselves were due some maintenance, and there was plenty of traffic, but we made good progress. None of the buildings around us were high and, like the road, all were due an overhaul. The colonial style, Victorian and Edwardian, was clear and beguiling - and crumbling. Colours were bright, but faded. Notices and advertising hoardings were everywhere, but few were in English. The main local language (over one hundred dialects are spoken in Burma, which is nothing if not a cultural melting pot) has 33 letters in its alphabet. Most of them appeared to be attractive shapes based on the Arabic letter O. It looked both fascinating and beautiful and reminded me of no other writing I have seen elsewhere. The overall effect of all this was intriguing. It was certainly less hectic than Bangkok, and had none of that city's high-rise and modern buildings; just a few smarter houses were interspersed with the others along the way. There were few traffic lights and where there were some they were strung on wires set high above the road.

We passed a huge lake and noticed that most of the roads were tree lined. This is in fact a pretty green city with many areas of open space. As we went towards the centre things got busier, and at least a few taller buildings appeared. The number of people about increased too and we saw shops, stalls, many with multicoloured umbrellas raised to protect them from the sun, and ample evidence of buying and selling, then we turned off into what Gi-Gi described as "the diplomatic district". We turned into a quiet narrower tree lined street of smart houses, and passed the embassy of India, housed in an imposing white building that looked like a smart country house. A couple of bored looking khaki-clad guards were visible outside holding rifles, but apart from them the place appeared deserted. Gi-Gi told us that she had "never seen a single person go in or come out". Either Indian/Burmese relations are non-existent or the leafy street contained something of a twilight zone. Round the corner and opposite a large and attractive colonial style house, which was the Sri Lankan Embassy, we turned into a short driveway and arrived at our hotel.

As we alighted alongside an arched, wooden gateway a gong, used to welcome every new arrival, sounded a deep boom and eager, welcoming staff clustered around, their smiles trained on us like searchlights. To enter the hotel you must walk along what is effectively a wooden bridge about forty metres long. It is open at the sides with the swimming pool on the left and ponds and gardens on the right, and is roofed to protect people in wet weather. As you walk along it, the Governor's Residence is visible in front of you, an imposing two story building, built more than one hundred years back in teak and with a distinct colonial style and open terraces all around the front. Since it became a hotel ten years ago, this has been *the* place to stay in Yangon if you want a taste of style and history. It is not large, having fewer than fifty rooms in a series of wooden buildings behind the main one, which simply houses a reception area, the restaurant, a pub-style bar and lounge. We were sat comfortably on the terrace and given a cool lemongrass tea as check-in procedures were quickly completed. Along the terrace each table had a small bowl on it with what looked like grass growing in it. We were later told that this was rice – "Our small fields, come back in two months and you can eat it". The place was tranquil and quiet, an oasis of calm only a few steps from the hubbub of the busy city.

The reception area was presided over by Thomas. He told me he had been with the hotel for ten years, and his effortless and urbane manner spoke of his years of experience. He would be a perfect candidate for any job involving smoothing ruffled feathers. There seemed to be no gaps between anything he did. His every task seemed to flow together into one smooth continuity of welcome and service and soon all the paperwork was done. Such people always seem to have some sort of internal air-conditioning too. You stand before them perspiring from every pore, rivulets of sweat trickling down your back and they appear to be standing in a different micro-climate, one that renders them cool in a way that should be physically impossible given the heat you are feeling. It is just one of life's little mysteries.

Our German travelling companions were similarly treated. The lady tried out a few words in English and seemed to discover with some pleasure that her schoolgirl language skills had begun to return. And in fact, she spent the rest of the trip speaking more and more as her vocabulary and her confidence grew. Each morning she greeted us at greater length and the comments she made about trips taken and sights seen increased too.

We were all shown to our respective rooms. Given enough beautiful wood you do not need much else to create something classy. The rooms were quietly understated; teak floors gave evidence of a hundred years of regular polishing, there were silk cushions and covers, tactile ceramics and locally painted pictures on the walls. Ours was comfortable, well-equipped and made a very good start to the visit. I could almost imagine ruling my own little part of India from a place like this. Well, perhaps ruling a small province. Once unpacked, we went to explore and have some lunch; Gi-Gi had explained that she would be back to collect us by mid-afternoon. In fact, a holiday this might be, a luxurious one at that, but a rest cure it would not prove to be. There was a great deal to see and our hosts were intent on making sure we saw as much as possible. For now we could relax, so we sat on the terrace alongside the swimming pool and enjoyed a light lunch. Trees surrounded the pool and its bottom was a random pattern of dark tiles so that it looked almost like a lake. Swimming in it later it felt rather like one too, and I half expected some toothy creature to emerge from a dark corner, pull me down and eat me. Despite this I completed a few lengths and emerged unscathed. Even monsters of the deep need a day off. During lunch there were more dragonflies than people about, bright translucent blue and green and so large one wondered how they could fly, but fly they did, patrolling low over the pool in graceful formation.

One thing I hate coming across when I travel abroad is people who seem to resent the locals and the local ways. Surely going abroad is, by definition, going to be somewhat different from staying at home. Something written by Dave Barry reflects this: "Americans who travel abroad for the first time are often shocked to discover that, despite all the progress that has been made in the last thirty years, many foreign people still speak a foreign language." I was reminded of this when we heard raised voices over by the reception desk. Although there is an Internet service in the country, it is offered by only one – Government – supplier, and most contact with the outside world is blocked. I had given it a try, trying to log into my email inbox as usual while travelling, but the screen showed only a brief message saying "Access

Denied", coupled with a warning phrase about prohibition and transgressing the system that had me quickly switching off. One more click and I might have found a man in black with a machine gun standing at my elbow This did not surprise me, since everything one read about travelling here mentioned it, but the American shouting angrily at the receptionist clearly had not done his homework. "What do you mean I can't use email?" he said. A long diatribe ensued during which he gave up on email and moved on to his mobile phone. "This is the latest technology, it will work anywhere in the world," he said, waving his phone about. Well, no - not here it won't. The receptionist had doubtless heard it all before. She struggled a little to find the right words in English, but managed to be patience personified. She sympathised, she explained; but he clearly felt he was the victim of a plot to curtail not just his business activities but also his liberty, and to say that he remained disgruntled is to understate his mood. Finally he gave up, saying "I suppose I'll just have to go use the satellite phone then" and, still muttering, stomped off to his room presumably to do just that. He seemed to travel well equipped, and for all I know he spent the rest of his stay bouncing laser signals off the moon to avoid enduring a single moment of isolation cut off from the United States.

Burma is a country that makes you very aware of its semi-isolation from the world at large. When I went to check for the stamps I needed to send a few postcards the receptionist told me, "They will take at least six weeks to arrive, better to send when you are back in Bangkok." It seemed like good advice and I followed it, so I can report nothing about the nature of Burmese postage stamps.

The General Manager here was Philippe Bissig. He was an experienced man and had previously run the very classy and much larger Sofitel Hotel in Thailand's coastal town of Hua Hin for some years. This is the large resort hotel in that town, which was once famous as the Railway Hotel before a big hotel group got their hands on it. It remains a special place and is renowned for serving an excellent English tea in its gardens. This was the place where once my wife opted to celebrate her birthday on a trip during which we crossed paths with Australian friends. Of course, running any hotel must be a full time job, yet here it must be a more relaxed position than at such a major property as the Sofitel. I could see any hotel manager being quite happy to see out their days in such a place.

The hotel garden acted as a luxury condominium for the local population of cicadas. The noise they made, a constant sound like dozens of women knitting in the distance, was relaxing rather than annoying, indeed it is a sound that occurs almost wherever you go in the East. We lazed, but not for long.

Chapter Four

Chapter Five

FIRST EXCURSIONS

"God made the country, and
man made the town."
William Cowper

There was a pleasant breeze to balance the heat and we could have happily sat on the terrace all day, but soon Gi-Gi was back and so was the mini-bus. Our first stop was one of Yangon's newer sights, the reclining Buddha at Kyaukhtatgyi Pagoda. Buddha figures abound all around this country and are usually found depicted in one of four positions or *asana*: reclining, standing, sitting crossed-legged or walking. Each reflects teaching or meditating except for reclining, which celebrates the Buddha's attainment of nirvana beyond death. Similarly the position in which the hands are placed is significant too. The right hand of a seated Buddha figure touching the ground while the left is across the lap is indicative of "calling the Earth to witness". If the thumb and forefinger of one hand form a circle, while the other hand has the fingers fanned out, the position symbolises the preaching of the first sermon. A raised right palm facing away from the body is evidence of displaying no fear. There are also meditation positions, which include the hands resting flat, one on top of the other in the lap and an offering position with the right hand palm up and parallel with the ground. Why the makers of most of the images picked one posture rather than another seems lost in the mists of time, but there is clearly more to the creation of such things than the designer's inspiration, as they reflect an age-old tradition and the details remain important long after the original construction.

At Kyaukhtatgyi more than 600 monks live in a monastery alongside the Buddha figure and busy themselves studying ancient Pali texts. Perhaps because large numbers of Buddhist monks were involved in the major protests in 1988 (indeed many were killed), the Buddhist order is now closely supervised by the government. Prospective monks, even those electing to stay for only a short time in a monastery, have to undergo a check before their ordination. I am not sure what this entails. Perhaps the authorities have some sort of reverence-ometer. But I doubt whether anyone so checked says they are going into a monastery to start a revolution, though many who do enter the monastic way of life may resent the junta as much as anyone. Permission must also be sought from the government before certain traditional ceremonies can be held, and monks may be pressed to influence people in the communities in which they live. It is even said that some monks are spies, wearing their robes only as a disguise to help them overhear things in circles to which they would otherwise have no access. While the monks here go about their business, alongside them the Buddha figure, its building financed by public donations just a few decades ago, keeps silent, enigmatic watch over their deliberations.

This is an imposing structure and the figure stretches out 70 metres in length. The first thing you see on arrival at such places is an array of shoes laid out on the ground outside. It might appear to be an incentive: visit our temple and you get a free pair of shoes. Actually, of course, they belong to people already inside. Every visitor must remove their shoes before they enter as a mark of respect. One sign at a temple read: "Foot wearing not allowed". Nearly always the second thing you will see close to the entrance are stalls selling a variety of trinkets apparently for locals and tourists alike. I saw no shoes for sale, so presumably those discarded during visits remain safe and are not stolen and need replacing. Even in sacred places commerce and culture rub shoulders with no apparent friction. In such a place you must also dress soberly. Shoulders must be covered, short skirts or shorts are not allowed and, should you transgress this rule, there will always be someone on hand to tell you and forbid entry until you don some of the additional garments usually kept at the entrance for just such a purpose. If you see any visitors who look like fashion disasters, dressed in ill matching clothes of clashing colours or from a bygone age, this probably is not their usual style at all. They are probably normally a picture of elegance, but just forgot to dress correctly for their visit and have had to cover up.

Gi-Gi checked our garb to ensure we were going to cause no offence, and walked us all round the huge figure. "This way to see backside," she told us and I could not resist pointing out that saying, "see other side" might risk less misunderstanding. Besides the figure was discretely robed. Around us numbers of local people knelt bowing their heads to the various images ranged around in a gesture called *shikoe* in which the head touches the ground. The huge Buddha figure had a bewildering array of symbols inscribed on the exposed soles of its massive feet, each one representing a different aspect of Buddhism. This huge effigy was housed rather incongruously under a tall, modern metal structure like an ugly farm building designed to store straw bales, it is actually called a *tazaung* or pavilion. Despite its housing, the figure was still impressive, and must have been a real sight when originally built and still uncovered so that it could be seen from the countryside around. Gi-Gi was dismissive about its huge size, explaining that there were three others in the country, all of which were bigger, "one much bigger."

We had both a formal tour of the city centre and time to make our own excursions. Familiar with other Asian cities – Singapore, Kuala Lumpur, Bangkok – Yangon by contrast seemed small to me; it was principally the lack of tall buildings and signs of cosmopolitan modernity that made it so different. It was a busy place, and every street seemed full of traffic and people and the noise and smells that accompanied this scene. Many people wore the traditional *longyis*, a skirt-like garment made from a two-metre-long panel of cloth knotted to secure it. Both men and women wore this simple garb, though strictly the women's version is called a *htamein* and the men's a *pasoe*. The sight of so many men in what appeared to be skirts seemed strange at first.

Around the Sule Pagoda, at 150 or so feet its gilded octagonal structure is the city's highest building set right in the city centre, tiny shops cluster in groups. First, a row of opticians. Then rows of shops printing photos, making signs and even similar premises displaying signs listing the doctors practising behind their narrow frontages. All the medics had impressive lists of letters after their names and their qualifications appeared to have been gained all over the world. How much this was a sign of true excellence is a moot point: here PhD is reputed to stand for phoney doctorate.

The British Embassy advice had been virtually to say, "if you go to Burma don't get sick." To this they might add, "If you do get sick choose your doctor wisely." All these groups offered a veritable surplus of choice. "How do people choose which establishment to use?" I asked Gi-Gi. "Oh, that's easy," she replied, "people just go to the one their grandfather patronised".

People here did not seem under any sort of threat, and certainly not an immediate one. The shops, their goods and displays spilling out onto the pavements, market stalls, food vendors whose mobile kitchens sent smoke and intriguing smells into the air around them, all seemed busy and to be doing a good trade. Many small shops seemed to have much of their wares laid out on canvas sheets on the pavement outside. In one long street the products displayed consisted almost entirely of books: new, second hand, and cheap, locally-produced copies. This was Pansodan Street, called *Lan-bay tekkatho* and referred to locally as the Sidewalk College. There were -plenty of English classics amongst the titles displayed too, and many old time heroes are evidently well read here. Sherlock Holmes is popular in English and in translation. Education may be a problem here but this was a clear sign that people wanted to read. Indeed more than 80% of the population of the country can read and write.

The book we saw most during the visit, one sold here and throughout the city and even from stalls in tiny villages, was George Orwell's *Burma Days*, a novel set in Burma and which surely owes its existence to the time he spent living in this country. It is the only one of his books you will see, however. The better known *1984* and *Animal Farm* are both banned; as they are believed to be inspired by unsavoury elements of the Burmese Government and even such classic literature is regarded as unsuitable for a population prevented from seeing even a single phrase of criticism about their rulers. Eric Blair, as George Orwell was named, lived in Burma in the 1920s and served in the police force founded by the British. It was a position that must have given him a unique insight into the Burma of those times.

Tea shops exist in abundance, the tea shop culture being very much part of Burmese life. Traditional Burmese tea is served in tiny cups. It is nowadays very sweet, as it is almost always made with condensed milk. People also eat tea, in the form of *lepet* or tea leaf salad; this consists of tea leaves packed into bamboo tubes, left to ferment and then mixed with sesame seeds and a little salt, chilli and lime juice and served with garnishes that might include garlic, shrimps, beans or peas. Coffee is also sweet and thick, and best only after the grounds have settled. It is not uncommon to see people make use of these meeting places and save money by ordering just a couple of teas, even though a group of eight or ten people may cluster round them. In such places people meet for breakfast on the way to work, for lunch and in the evening. Mostly providing seating on tiny low plastic stools, tea shops act as social exchanges for news and gossip as well as a place to meet friends. With the press heavily censored, any clue to what is really happening can only be picked up informally; doing so over a cup of tea or coffee in these cheerful emporiums is a necessary and enjoyable part of life. The local term for the informal news and gossip reflects this: they are referred to as Tea shop vapours. These establishments also act as movie theatres, with televisions and DVD players installed to show the latest films.

Understandably, action movies with minimal dialogue are the most popular of the international films, though locally produced films are, of course, in Burmese. It is said that government spies, that is agents of the DDSI (the Directorate of Defence Services), mix with people in such establishments ready to report anyone questioning government policy, passing on inappropriate news or simply recounting an inappropriate joke. No story here begins, "There was an Englishman, a Frenchman and a Burmese general." Given what I heard at Burma Campaign UK, I don't doubt that there is spying. But whatever care people were exercising as we went by, sounds of laughter predominated and people seemed happy. Life goes on and many people evidently ignore wider and political issues and just concentrate on their day-to-day life, one apparently that allows ample time for socialising.

In the United Kingdom one of the banes of modern life is chewing gum. Well, not the gum itself, rather the propensity for a certain category of mindless gum chewer, a numerous group too it must be said, to spit it out onto the pavement. As a result, most city pavements are spotted and look like they have some sort of disease. The long discarded pieces dry and bond themselves to the paving stones needing effort and cost to remove them. The newer ones, of course, bond themselves to your shoes. They then get trodden into the house and drive those of a curmudgeonly disposition like myself into demented outbursts about the state of society, and boost the profits of carpet cleaning firms around the country. In Burma the equivalent of this is betel. This is the Areca or Pinang nut. The leaves are smeared with lime, wrapped around sliced nuts, spiced with fennel seeds and cloves or dried liquorish shreds. It is chewed for its mildly euphoric stimulant effect. It is addictive and thus widespread, and so are the red splatters it leaves on the ground when its users spit out the chewed up remnants. It looks thoroughly unpleasant and stains the teeth of those using it a deep, bright red that makes them look like vampires; in fact maybe some of them are vampires and remain undetected only by hiding evidence of their nocturnal hobby by chewing betel. It is also thought to be carcinogenic and has various other unpleasant side effects such as irritating asthma. Still it is popular, though gradually its use is declining. It is reputed to have a few beneficial effects; for instance tapeworms don't like it much, so a few of its adherents may take it for medicinal purposes. It is also supposed to reduce anaemia in pregnancy, though the horrendous look it produces in the mouths of its users would surely be an effective contraceptive and stop any chance of pregnancy dead in its tracks. It must be a regular occurrence here to spot someone you fancy, get them to smile at you and then find that all lustful thoughts evaporate as they expose their teeth. No one knows betel's origins, the first known signs of human habitation in Burma date from about 9000 BC and, who knows, the people back then might have been characterised by their red mouths. Anyway, it is a constant presence in the streets and while Singapore, renowned for fining people for a long list of indiscretions, has simply banned chewing gum to remove the problems that it causes, there is no sign of the same thing happening here with regard to betel. It is as ubiquitous as the large, loosely-rolled Burmese cheroots, which are widely smoked around the country. It pays to mind your step here.

At one point we got a taxi to the city's main market. Scotts Market, now correctly called the much less catchy name of Bogyoke Aung San Market, is on the corner of Sule Pagoda Road and Bogyoke Aung San Street just north of the Indian and Chinese areas of shops in the city centre. Taxis have no meters so it pays to have an idea how far you are going and how much it might reasonably cost. The driver we found, who was parked just across the road from the hotel entrance, spoke some English and told me with some pride that the aged Toyota car he drove was "Really quite new – only built in 1984." That was ten years before the *Road to Mandalay* was upgraded and they had had to spend US$ 6 million to get that right. The car did not look as if it had had as much as a dollar spent on it since it was imported. When he started it up there was a pause before the engine hesitatingly got going. It was a bit like calling an extremely elderly dog to go for a walk. Wave the lead and call "walk" and it will at once give you a pleased look, but it then takes a moment to heave itself upright and make for the front door. Nonetheless, and despite the driver sitting on the wrong side of the car given the side of the road he needed to drive on, once he was under way he whisked us safely through the city streets to our destination. Our safety was more likely down to the lucky red ribbons hanging from his rear view mirror than his maintenance programme. He charged exactly what we had been told he should.

The market was in a main street off the city centre. Our driver dropped us off and we walked the last few hundred metres towards it alongside buildings predominantly rendered and painted in a variety of colours. Narrow side streets run away from the main road with buildings maybe four or five stories high that obviously contained apartments. Washing hung out on balconies and at open windows, satellite dishes adorned the roofs, spaghettis of electric wires linked the two sides of the street and people scurried to and fro beneath. Lines hung from some of the windows and were clearly used to get things upstairs: as I watched someone attached a basket to one of them, shouted up to the window and watched as it was hoisted aloft. The market was housed in a pink painted concrete building topped with small towers and had stalls spread over two floors. It sold everything you can think of: food, clothes, ornaments, household goods and more. Amongst the more everyday things on display, almost anything you looked at showed evidence of the country's poor economy. Shirts for instance were only a dollar or two each and the cotton material was rough and basic. There were better quality items in some places and my wife negotiated with two rival, but apparently co-operating, stall holders to buy pashminas, afterwards failing to make me understand why the only way to get a good deal was to buy three of them. The local currency is the *kyat* (unaccountably pronounced as "chat"). Dollars are used alongside them as a sort of sub currency, and certainly when approaching foreigners a dollar price always seemed to be offered first. It was illegal to change money other than through official channels – the rate was about 1200 *kyats* for one U.S. dollar - but nevertheless people offering to make an unofficial exchange regularly and openly approached us throughout our visit. The exchange rate they offered was barely different from the official one, so fearful of the consequences for both parties, I played safe and stuck to the official channels. One sign of the government's mismanagement of the economy is that inflation is rife; many things, including the thousands of bicycles we saw around us are bought and then resold as their price rises. Put money in the bank and a year later it is worth 25% less and will only buy you the bike's front wheel, tuck a whole bicycle away ready to resell later and your savings are safe.

Although there were very few westerners around in the streets or markets the atmosphere certainly seemed friendly and unthreatening. Gi-Gi had confidently sent us off on our own without a qualm. English speaking was somewhat restricted, but where they could, people seemed to enjoy talking with us. A small boy of maybe ten or eleven years approached us at one point, explained that he was learning English at school and wanted to speak with us. He spoke pretty well too and told me that when he grew up he wanted to be a scientist. If speaking English helped he was well on his way, but few people aspired to such things; or rather few people were in a position to aspire to such things. Gi-Gi told me later that it was likely that his family had money and that he attended a private school. This prompted me to ask about something to do with education that was obviously rather politically sensitive. Gi-Gi was not embarrassed or evasive, but she smiled, ignored the question completely and changed the subject. "Let me tell you about..." It was a tactic that I saw repeated a number of times. Presumably she was in too obvious contact with foreigners for her not to be careful; it is said Burma is the only country where the police are more dangerous than the animals in the zoo. Other people wanted to make a point, many stallholders told us, "good you come here" and made it clear that we should tell others to come too. But most were less forthcoming. It reminded me of a story I had heard as I checked things out before leaving

England: a Burmese manages to travel from his hometown to Yangon and then on to Bangkok where he visits a dentist. "Don't you have dentists in Burma?" the dentist asks him. "Oh, yes," he replies, "but we are not allowed to open our mouths."

One afternoon we had time for a walk around Kandawgyi (it means Royal Lake) and strolled along the wooden walkways that surround much of its shore. This is one of many park areas within the city. At one end of the lake the floating Karaweik Restaurant dominates the scene. This is a huge wooden barge modelled on the *pye-gyi-mun* vessel belonging to Burmese royalty. It has a double bow, depicting a mythological water bird, the *Karaweik*, and the restaurant is housed above decks in a structure like a multi-tiered pagoda. In the evening we took the same taxi driver who had earlier taken us to the market and went to see the famous Strand Hotel, intending to have something to eat there. This is near the river in a square alongside the Independence Monument, an obelisk 150 feet high surrounded by five smaller pillars representing Burma's five once-virtually autonomous States: Shan, Kachin, Kayah, Kayin, and Chin. The Strand is Yangon's grandest hotel, built in 1901 by a British entrepreneur, John Darwood, and later acquired by the famous Sarkies brothers, who, amongst other places owned Raffles Hotel in Singapore. In its heyday it was the height of grandeur, and in 1911 Murray's Handbook described it as, "patronised by royalty, nobility and distinguished personages". It has had its ups and downs, including being bombed during World War II, when a bomb hit what is now the manager's office, failed to explode, but sat there for some days before being removed. Business went on as usual while it lay there. The building's colonial exterior and the inside were renovated in the early 1990's, and its 100 or so rooms are now all smart suites. The entrance and the main lounge it leads into are certainly impressive. You can look up an atrium to the two floors above, and it is furnished in style with wicker chairs and traditional eastern décor.

The bar, which we went to for a drink, was somewhat less appealing, being an awkward L-shaped space rather like a narrow old style railway waiting room. We ordered a drink – it was Friday evening and the happy hour deal offered drinks at half price. Soon, at 6-30, background pop music began playing at a level that was distinctly obtrusive. We asked if we could take our drinks to the lounge, got grudging agreement, but no help was offered to carry things through. A man at the bar's door asked what the problem was and when I explained he said only, "What's the matter, don't you like music?" The lounge was more pleasant, but service was hardly much in evidence. I asked at the desk for a hotel brochure and was given a one-page fact sheet. Then I saw someone who was clearly a manager, and asked him if they did not have a proper brochure; he went to the desk and came back with something much more professional and informative, which he gave me before hurrying away. As we sat three separate couples came in, sat down and then, having been ignored for ten minutes or more, they ordered nothing and left muttering. The manager, to whom I had explained my need for a brochure by saying that I was to write something about my visit, then returned and offered me a look at one of the hotel's suites, handing over abruptly to one of the reception staff who duly toured me round but displayed little interest or enthusiasm. The rooms were certainly impressive, and at a cost of between US$ 400 and US$900 per night well they might be, but the service was distinctly lack lustre to put it mildly. It is said that hotel staff can be in trouble with the military if they become too friendly with guests, but surely here they were opting for the wrong extreme. I asked for the check and was not only mischarged for the drinks, but also had a disingenuous squabble to get the matter put right. Perhaps we were just not the kind of "distinguished personages" they were used to. Be that as it may, somewhat disillusioned, we decided to ignore their smart restaurants and went back to eat at the Governor's Residence, well pleased that we had chosen this much more appealing place to stay.

The restaurant was usually empty here in the evening, not because there is anything wrong with it but because its seating flows out onto the terrace and on into the garden and everyone seemed to prefer to be seated outside, as did we. Every evening as dusk fell a line of patterned umbrellas were set up around the garden's edge. Laid on their sides in front of lamps that illuminated them from behind, they formed an unusual and attractive backdrop for an evening meal. Before dinner one evening I went to the upstairs lounge, a lofty room open to the air at the front and overlooking the garden. This offers music and dancing to accompany pre-dinner drinks, which can be taken sitting on huge comfortable wicker chairs. Four musicians performed, led by an uncharacteristically fat lady, who I unkindly christened Blancmange Woman, as much because of her billowing, multi-layered pink party dress, the kind of thing ten-year olds used to love to wear, as because of her size. They played lilting local music and accompanied two costumed dancers –

a man and a woman. I was there for a drink while my wife changed for dinner. Few other people were in the lounge and the dancers came and did an individual turn in front of each of us. I tried to suggest to one of them that, in my case, she should wait a moment until my wife came, but the dancer did not understand. She did though evidently pass on the fact that I had made a comment, because moments later Blancmange Women hastened over to see what I had wanted. Later, when most people went to dinner, she ensconced herself on what I imagined must have been a small stool in the garden and played, rather nicely, on a harp. Her substantial skirts hid the stool completely so that she appeared to be suspended in the air. Traditionally it is said that something is not over until the fat lady sings; that did not happen here, she did not sing, but continued to play until dinner was finished.

The service here was everything that at the Strand Hotel it was apparently not: stylish, efficient and charming. Only once during our stay did English fail in a brief misunderstanding, until a second waitress promptly appeared to combine her language skills with her colleague's and all was quickly sorted out. The atmosphere here was magic. In the evening the ponds around the garden had candles floated on them, the temperature was pleasant as the heat of the day declined and there was no unpleasant humidity. The busy city, actually only a few streets distant, seemed miles away.

The most unmissable sight in Yangon is the Schwedagon Pagoda. Described by Somerset Maugham as looking "... like a sudden hope in the dark night of the soul...", it is said to have more gold spread about its person than there is in the Bank of England. The ratio is probably increasing day by day, as the present government seems to rather like selling British gold, usually when the market for it is low and the financiers howl with laughter all the way to the bank. The stupa is plated with nearly 9000 solid gold slabs and its huge bell-shaped tower, the top part is called the *zedi*, rises some 100 metres above the city. The opulence is staggering: high up to catch the sun are set more than 5000 diamonds and 2000 rubies, and all around, spread across 14 acres, more than 100 additional surrounding buildings, including 64 smaller stupas, are ranged alongside and beautifully decorated. This structure goes way back, its origins unknown but probably more than 2000 years ago. It is recorded that it was well established in the 11th century and has been added to and suffered from Burma's turbulent history ever since. For example, the British tried to take one of its many huge bells away to Calcutta during their 1824 – 1826 occupation, but they only succeeded in allowing it to sink to the bottom of the river – all thirty tons of it. The local people managed to raise it when the British promised that if they did so it could be returned to its home. The British insensitively removed a great many artefacts during their rule. Some were returned in more enlightened times, and some of those are still referred to in a way that recalls this history; so what is called a returned–Buddha is a much travelled one and has probably been to India, or even Europe, and back again during its life. Schwedagon has also suffered damage by fire and earthquake. Whatever has befallen it, local people have always somehow raised the money to restore it and it certainly remains most impressive today; walking around its main platform puts one in awe of the time, effort and cost creating such a place represents. The Buddhist way, incidentally, is for people always to walk clockwise around such structures, as doing so puts your heart closest to it.

Tourists and local people alike come to visit. We saw many locals paying their respects at specific shrines, lighting candles or pouring water over small statues using a metal ladle. In one quiet corner is a *Bondhi* tree. The Buddha is said to have sat under such a tree when he was enlightened so long ago, and this one is said to have been grown from a cutting of the actual tree Buddha sat under on that fateful day. It stands majestically amidst the buildings, with its curious twisted trunk and leaves giving shade. In England only a minority of people now subscribe to a religion. As a result many a church has a permanent campaign going on to save its crumbling roof or spire, and it is a battle to get anyone outside its often small congregation, people or government, to contribute care or resources sufficient to maintain such buildings. Yet here in such a poor country, massive amounts of money seem to be donated and put into the upkeep of religious buildings, temples and shrines of all sorts. Schwedagon is truly impressive, both as a building and as a sign of the commitment of local people to their heritage.

All too soon it was time to move on. We enjoyed a final breakfast on the terrace and, packed and ready for the continuing journey, our little group were met at the front of the hotel again by the ever-smiling Gi-Gi who was all set to get us onto the flight to Bagan.

Chapter Five

Chapter Six

ALL ABOARD

"We wander for distraction, but
we travel for fulfilment."
Hilaire Belloc

It was mini bus time again and Gi-Gi expertly shepherded her charges – there were now eight of us – from the hotel to Yangon's small airport. Small it may have been, but that morning it was chaotic. Everything was organised for us, however, and as we waited a few moments just inside the terminal, our luggage was whisked away and boarding passes were handed over. One of Gi-Gi's colleagues had done the queuing for us; what a job, I hope he had a suitably impressive title, Vice-President Queuing, perhaps. We could not avoid the wait that followed, however, and sat in a long stuffy room on fixed plastic chairs as the crowds grew around us. There were few western faces to be seen. Being near the glass wall at the front we found we could see our suitcases, first being thrown with huge gusto onto a trolley and then, buried by others and wheeled away to the plane. Finally boarding was announced. The announcement took the form of someone holding a crumpled piece of cardboard aloft with the flight number written on it and waving it about in a please follow-me kind of way. A bus took us to the plane, which was waiting only a few hundred metres away. It was a twin-propped aircraft of uncertain vintage, designed to carry a hundred or so people and operated by Air Mandalay. Nearby a similar plane bore the Myanmar Airways logo. The British Embassy may have banned its staff from flying on that airline, but it apparently remained busy and operational despite their disfavour. What is more, livery apart, we appeared to be going on a similar plane.

Now my attitude is simple: if I was frightened of flying I would not fly. I assume the pilot wants to land safely as much as I do and do not worry about it. My wife on the other hand dislikes it. She puts up with it because she likes to travel, but likes her planes big, shiny, new and powered by jet engines, preferably ones with the words Rolls Royce written on the side; not least because her engineer father once worked for that august company. This plane was the antithesis of that. It was clearly not new, it had two propellers and it went down the runway for takeoff rather like an uncertain crab, seeming to go sideways as much as forwards. Despite this it did manage to get itself airborne and soon settled into a reasonably smooth and straight course. The flight was only an hour and I did hand-holding duties; it is a fact that I did not appreciate before meeting my wife that holding hands makes a successful takeoff or landing very much more likely. After an hour of uneventful flight she was doing a good imitation of being calm as we landed; then we came down like the proverbial ton of bricks, a process that was sufficiently unnerving to be accompanied by gasps from many of the passengers. The tannoy announcement said, "We have now landed in Bagan"; but we *knew*, we already knew. We were safe and sound but I felt it did not bode well for the journey back. Actually the plane was a product of ATR, a French-Italian consortium (Aerei da Transporto or Avions de Transport according to taste) formed in 1981. This kind of plane first flew in 1988 and some 800 are in service with more than 150 operators around the world. I suspect this one was made early in their life, in which case it may have the unusual feature of needing a tail stand: that's something to stop the nose rising off the ground as passengers get on board, as they must, through the rear door. That apart, their record is generally good and none have crashed since 2005 when one went down in the Mediterranean. I made a point of not telling my wife this, 2005 was not so long ago, and I massaged my hand back to life as we collected our bags.

As this was an internal flight, there were no customs or passport people for us to contend with, so we were soon through the chaos of an airport even smaller than Yangon's and on our way to a small bus. The luggage we presumed to be safe. Gi-Gi had said to us, "Not to worry, you will next see it on the ship". We had seen luggage unloading from the plane as we disembarked so assumed all would be well. Our guide for the next few days met us. San appeared to be in his mid-late thirties and had worked for *Road to Mandalay* for ten years. He had a neat moustache and a beard trimmed to cover just his chin. He projected calm and enthusiasm in equal measure, and was to prove a delightful and knowledgeable guide. We were, he told us, only twenty minutes from the ship, a number of people from the flight were transferring and we were to go to one of three buses, ours labelled "English 1". Our new German friend could stop struggling with her English for a moment and get on the bus with the German speaking guide.

The road was fair if a little rough and rather surprisingly was partly dual carriageway. The mix of traffic was light and we passed a horse and trap, several bullock carts laden with vegetables and some foreign tourists on bicycles as well as the usual aged cars. The empty countryside was arid and cultivation sparse. Suddenly one passenger swatted at a small fly and San gently reminded us that in a Buddhist country all life was sacred. "Mind you," he continued, "some people will kill an annoying mosquito, but be careful - kill one and a thousand more may come to its funeral." Yes, that could be even more annoying. Introductions continued as we progressed and in what seemed like moments we were turning off the road onto a track, past a few buildings and a rundown looking temple and driving towards the river. This was the dry season in an arid part of the country and, like all the traffic here, the buses kicked up clouds of dust from the rough roads, and this intensified as we took to the track. A few minutes later we pulled up at a huddle of buildings and could see the river below us. We walked around the building and the view was spectacular. The river was wide – maybe a mile across – and the main channel had a visible flow to it, otherwise it looked calm and serene with the water brightly sparkling in the sunlight. A twisting flight of steps led down to the ship and beyond that a gangplank led across on board.

The ship was predominantly white and shone in the bright sunlight. She was secured to her mooring by four long, thick ropes, three secured in one direction holding her against the current. Beyond her, in the main channel, small boats could be seen and a barge carrying logs was pulled past by another boat, secured to its side, which looked two sizes too small for the job. We would see many of these log carriers as Burma is half covered with tropical forest and produces three quarters of the world's teak. Much of the logging work is still done using elephants, of which there are more than 10,000 in Burma including those living wild. Once trees are felled and sawed into sections these are dragged out of the forest by trained elephants. It is a method that does little damage to the forest and an elephant can access areas that would defeat even the most modern tractor. They push, pull and generally manoeuvre the logs down to the river where waterpower takes over. The training of elephants, whether bred for work or captured, is carefully controlled. Full training takes many years and the *usi* or handlers look after a valuable investment as well as keeping this tradition of working elephants alive and helping with one of Burma's main industries, one that is increasingly organised to be properly sustainable.

We made our way down the path, across the gang plank and on board to be warmly greeted by some of the crew, one of whom ticked our names off on a list at the reception desk in the area we had come into and showed us to our cabin. As we walked into it we could see through the window a surprisingly small boat pulling alongside with our luggage piled high on board. A few minutes later the suitcases caught us up and were delivered to the cabin.

The cabin was a good size, more like a small, comfortable and good quality hotel room than a ship's cabin. It had everything one needed: a large double bed, wardrobes, a unit at the foot of the bed with a television on it, and a neat and surprisingly spacious en-suite bathroom with a shower. These days many people would regard somewhere with no television as distinctly sub-standard. Here however we were to be much too busy to resort to the programme of in-house movies or whatever channels it might be able to pick up; the television was surely strictly for night owls or those uninterested in their surroundings. We unpacked and went up two decks (there were four) to the dining room where a buffet lunch was spread out. Most tables were arranged around the outside of the room and we were able to sit by a large window with a view across the river. We also began to meet some of the other passengers in our very cosmopolitan group. Amongst others we met two American women, Lillian and Sandy, travelling together, New Yorkers Alan and Sue, who currently lived in Hong Kong, a couple from Melbourne, four people from Norway who told us there was two metres of snow at home, and more – from Brazil, England, France and Germany. All were first-time visitors except one, returning after a first visit more than twenty years back. Many people were, as we discovered, regular travellers, though no one we talked to beat a record San told us about later, a recent lady passenger had ticked off visiting her 160th country by coming to Burma, all in 14 years since retiring. What a race that must have been. Maybe in some of them she stopped long enough to enjoy a cup of tea. Sounds expensive too, I wonder who arranged her retirement pension; perhaps she bumped off her husbad for the insurance and travelled to avoid the body under the patio.

After lunch we had an opportunity to see something of Bagan before the ship headed for Mandalay, which it would not do until the next day. Bagan was built around the 11th century, so missed being listed as one of the ancient wonders of the world, but it is regarded as Burma's most amazing sight and on a par with many other classic world treasures such as the Taj Mahal in India. The remains of the ancient Buddhist city cover 40 square kilometres on a flat plane forming the east bank of the Ayeyarwady River. All the buildings except the religious monuments were built of wood and have vanished long ago, and only the brick, sandstone and stucco of the temples and pagodas have survived. It its heyday it must have been something to behold. With its many towers originally covered in gold or silver, Marco Polo called them "... one of the finest sights in the world... when illuminated by the sun they are especially brilliant and can be seen from a great distance." He described the whole city as, "A gilded city, alive with tinkling bells and the swishing sounds of monks' robes." It is reckoned that over a period of two hundred years or so, starting from about the year 1050, over 13,000 temples, pagodas and other religious buildings were erected. Now only some 2000 remain, though evidence of many more is there in ruins. The city is sometimes said to have been sacked by invading Mongols, but its decline was in fact more gradual. Some buildings were demolished by the Burmese to build defences; more simply fell and disappeared as a result of neglect over the turbulent years that followed the time of their building. The fact that this is an active earthquake zone was doubtless significant too; a large shock happened as recently as 1975. I realised thinking about this that I had not included a check on the kind of frequency with which earthquakes strike here in my earlier research. I hoped it was at least comparatively rare, but there was something else to worry about; and rightly so, as I discovered later.

Today the main town nearby is Nyaung U, which acts as the centre of what is called the Bagan Archaeological Zone. This is a place that does act to produce revenue for the government as it costs US$ 10 for someone to enter. On a tour like ours, of course, the guide will see to this and many tourists may not even notice that this is done as the charge will have been added into the total cost of their trip. San marshalled his small flock and we set off to see something of the surrounding countryside. Our first stop was Ananda Temple.

This is an impressive structure; its whitewashed façade dominates the village on its northern edge. Again this is an ancient structure, being completed in 1091. It is what is called a corridor temple, its ground plan in the shape of a cross, with four large halls linking to entrances on each of the four sides, which in this case are more than 50 metres in length. Four niches house tall Buddha images, lit from openings high in the roof, and almost 10 metres high. Two of the figures are original. Two are copies replacing the original figures, which were stolen. Theft and desecration have been a problem throughout the ages, and many Buddha images have damage around the stomach where thieves have smashed them to try and find any valuables hidden within. As time passed we saw many such statues and images, with a number protected behind metal bars or secured in glass cases. San showed us an optical illusion. As one looked at one of the Buddha figures through the arch of the entrance hall in front of it, it appeared to be smiling, as you moved forward the smile appeared to flatten. It was said he told us, "... that in ancient times only royalty were allowed to approach closely, so the smile is for the common people, but not for kings". Once one noticed it, the effect was pronounced. It would literally have been possible to spend many days visiting different temples and still leave many unseen. A temple here is not a place of worship. Buddha is not regarded as a god, and a temple is thus primarily a place of meditation. I discovered that the word pagoda referred to the characteristic shape involved, somewhat reminiscent of a pyramid at its base, topped with an elegant bell-shaped tower, the very topmost part of which I mentioned earlier is called a *zedi*. A pagoda is something people could enter, but a stupa is solid with no entrance, though often religious relics of some sort are thought to have been placed at the centre and then bricked in. Again this fact has attracted thieves over the years and at least some of them have succeeded in tunnelling in and locating treasure. Buddhism has always had a hold on the population here and Burma is often referred to as the most Buddhist country in the world, but there are clearly some who are prepared to leave its precepts on one side for the sake of a quick profit.

The largest structures have sometimes achieved their size by repeatedly being extended as someone has built another layer on top of the original structure. It is believed that one earns merit, and a chance of a better future life, by undertaking good and reverent deeds. Building these sorts of places is regarded as such a deed, so in part the numbers involved represents this constant striving. There was also an element of keeping up with the Joneses: if you are going to build something, then what you build must outshine others. Merit and the search for it are inherent to the Buddhist way of life. It is a little like having a bank account, you deposit a kind of spiritual capital in it and then draw on your savings using what you've accumulated as a deposit on a better life next time round. Merit can be gained in all sorts of ways, many of them linked to monks. You gain merit by helping the monks collect their food, or donating in other ways: with robes for monks or money to help upkeep temples, or even just by congratulating other people for doing similar things. Compared with the West, that sounds an easier way to keep up with the Joneses than buying something that will make their new BMW look hopelessly uninteresting. Although some Buddhists literally see all this as an end in its own right and carry a notebook to keep a running check on their karmic "score", this is not really the point. Merit is gained only as a by-product of doing what is right, and just doing deeds solely to gain merit is self-defeating as with such a motivation it scores you few points. It is all a little complicated, but the "doing the right thing" side of things is something that commends Buddhism to many people. It all reminds me of one of those unanswerable questions, like why does the partner who snores always go to sleep first? And why is abbreviated such a long word? In this case the question that asks: why do people who believe in reincarnation bequeath their money to other people?

In another temple, with a dark interior because it was virtually without windows, we saw that almost the entire inside surface was covered with elaborate murals; people, animals and scenes of town and country were virtually wall to wall and rose high overhead. San shone a lamp for us. The quality of what remained varied. In some places the full pictures had survived, in others they were faded so as to be almost invisible with just a few tantalising shapes hinting at the glory and colours of centuries ago. In nearby Nandamannya Temple, murals are rather different in nature. Actually they consist of erotic paintings depicting the daughters of Mara attempting to seduce the Buddha. Their nubile figures appear to be going about it with expertise and vigour, but it was doubtless to no avail and the Buddha resisted their charms.

Although we could have spent all of our limited time in temples and visiting pagodas, there were other things to see and our next stop was a lacquerware factory. Like so much else, lacquerware was invented in China in the 11th century. It did not make such a satisfying a bang as gunpowder did, but it was quickly developed into a real art form. Burma is famous for it, and for the quality of its workmanship. Although wood is sometimes used as a base for the trays, bowls and vases that are typical of this work, the best lacquer ware has a core of shaved bamboo strips, a light bamboo lattice that gives flexibility. Strips are cut from the bamboo and literally woven into the shape required. The raw lacquer is a resin that is taken from the *thitsi* tree, rather as latex rubber is tapped. This murky sticky stuff turns black on exposure to air and is spread over the core bowl or whatever is being made. It sets hard and is then polished to the characteristically smooth and tactile lacquer finish. Many layers are commonly applied to create good quality items, as many as 26 being quoted as the maximum. The production process can thus last several months. Then the finished product, still jet black, can be engraved, painted and given a final polish. The prevailing Buddhist influence is often evident, with designs featuring life-cycle stories or celestial animals and mythological figures. The end result can be stylish and beautiful and the texture of lacquer is unique and very tactile.

Within the small factory we visited, spread through four or five ramshackle rooms, two or three dozen people were at work. One could see every stage of the process, from making the original shape to adding the lacquer, polishing and decorating. It was painstaking work that clearly had to be executed with great skill. We wandered round and spoke to some of the workers, who were mostly women. One girl, who I would guess was only in her twenties, and was engraving a bowl, told me that she earned 1000 *kyat* per day. That's not quite as much as a single American dollar, but then annual incomes here are on average very low for most people, with, say, a hotel worker away from the main tourist areas only earning four or five thousand *kyats* a month. She seemed to take great pride in her work, and the finished items, while some would probably not mix with western styles, were mostly very beautiful. I can see a stunning lidded bowl, which I bought as a reminder of the trip, sitting close by where I am writing this. It is still something I not only admire, but which I have to touch on a regular basis. I probably appreciate it more now I know how long and painstaking was the process of producing it.

Late in the afternoon, we stopped briefly in a small village on our way to another pagoda. It consisted of simple wooden houses, some little more than bamboo and thatch huts. One "house" was often a cluster of smaller buildings and San told us that different rooms were often built intentionally separate. "This way, if the kitchen catches fire the whole house is not burned down." People cook entirely on charcoal or wood, so the danger is doubtless ever present. From here they worked the arid land around. Plums from a huge pile lay out on a canvas sheet, and were being sorted and packed by a circle of squatting villagers to be exported to China. Goats wandered amongst the buildings and children played, running hither and thither amongst all the activity or were busy doing their share of the chores. Women walked gracefully carrying enormous bundles on their heads. It was not quite like the Middle Ages, but we were certainly not in Kansas anymore. Everyone appeared to be working happily together and although I could understand little of what people were saying, the sound of laughter is universal and there was plenty of that. I thought of one of the things that Mark, who I had met at Burma Campaign UK, had told me, that government and military people could descend on such a village to recruit a work party. People would have to drop everything and go off to repair a road or whatever the project was, they would be fed, but not paid and might be away a day, a week or a year. Complaining was not an option, and presumably a measured amount of forced labour was better than the spell in an unsavoury prison, which any resistance would certainly mean. There might be little sign of such activity visible to visitors, but that did not mean it was not there. So many are involved that most people are said to know someone who is directly affected.

For protection the people will often hang a coconut from the eves in the South East corner of their home to honour the Min Mahagir or house *nat* and to afford some protection in their lives. Burmese Buddhism goes hand in hand with animism, and the *nats* are believed to be spirits, inhabiting almost every aspect of the landscape, a belief in them stemming from pre-Buddhist cultures. Images of *nats* often decorate temples. Wherever they are, they are regularly honoured. Gifts of food and flowers are set out where they are believed to be or by their man made images, especially on special occasions, to ensure that they do not forget to protect people, a community or an individual, from everything from wild animals to sickness and thieves. It appears to be a simple philosophy: look after your *nat* and your *nat* will look after you. There are thirty-seven main *nats*, all with their own names and history, and many more minor ones. This is surely enough to ward off almost everything unpleasant, though they presumably draw the line at military juntas. Mount Popo, a volcanic peak ring five hundred metres above the plain south of Pakokku, part of which is now a wild life sanctuary, is regarded as their principle home. As such it is the site of many shrines in their honour. At full moon in December and June there are major festivals held there in their honour. These festivals attract thousands of pilgrims and show how the old animistic beliefs still exist and how they somehow fit in alongside Buddhism. I am not sure whether *nats* are inclined to travel, and of course export of religious images is forbidden, but perhaps one situated at the South East corner of my house might slow the wind that seems to take out at least one stretch of fencing every winter. This usually happens when I am away, and a good neighbour scurries round to secure it (thank you, Ron). Lillian, one of the two Americans we had met, had a particular fascination with the *nats*. San responded to her questions with stories and background. For instance, retelling the legend of Mahagiri Nat, about a brother and sister. A king, Thinlikyaung, fell for and married the sister despite regarding the popularity of her brother as a threat to his kingship. Hounded because of this, the brother had hidden in the forest, but returned after the marriage when the king promised to spare him. The king, however, immediately had him seized, tied to a tree and burnt. His sister, horrified at seeing this, threw herself into the flames and was killed too. Brother and sister became *nats* and lived in the *saga* tree. The king ordered the tree cut down and thrown in the river. Later as the story of their deaths spread, the king had the tree retrieved and images of the two *nats* were carved from the wood and placed in a shrine.

In the early evening we were out on the Bagan plain, and had climbed high up on a semi-ruined stupa. The view across the flat plain, initially still shimmering from the heat of the day, was stunning in every direction. There were no crowds to dilute the stillness and quiet. The entire landscape was studded with the shapes of towers of all sizes, and between them ruins of other buildings showed clearly the extent of such buildings that had once covered the plain. There must have been hundreds still standing within view and they stretched 360 degrees around as far as the eye could see. This was the sort of sight that, however many pictures you have seen, however much you have read about it, the reality makes prior imaginings pale into utter insignificance. It was awe-inspiring and somehow dreamlike. It was humbling to imagine, as one could, this scene in its prime: the pagodas pristine and shining gold, wooden buildings filling the gaps between them to form a city, smoke rising from fires and people going about their everyday business. As a place to observe a sunset it is difficult to imagine anywhere better. One modern building showed in the distance. Not yet complete, this was a new viewing platform designed to provide a vantage point for tourists who do some damage climbing up and down the old buildings. However necessary, I do not think it will provide the same experience and I was glad to see the scene ahead of this tower being finished. Its modern stark silhouette stood out amongst the ruins and did nothing for the view. The sun sank, the sky turned red and the misty haze on the horizon swallowed the sun's blood red globe before it reached the horizon itself. We climbed back down to the ground and as we went slowly back to the ship, people were quiet and reflective. Understandably so. It is a sight I will remember for a very long time.

Later Myo Aye Khine ("Meo"), a beautiful Burmese staff member, delivered us drinks on the open top deck of the ship before dinner. The sun had now set, but her smile lit up the deck and made us feel most welcome. While sitting there I made a surprising and important discovery. Huge. Momentous. All tea, coffee, soft drinks and, wait for it... beer, were *free* on board. It was mentioned in a small footnote to the drinks menu. They were all free. I can understand the tea and so on, but I don't think I have ever been anywhere where free beer was the norm before. What a treat! I promptly had a second one to celebrate. Burmese beer is, I had discovered at the Governor's Residence, pretty limited. There seemed to be three brands, all lager: Mandalay beer in two strengths and Myanmar beer. In my youth the brewery local to where I lived sold a beer that was popularly described as tasting "better coming up than going down". These were not like that, but all were rather lacklustre and frankly impossible to tell apart. I settled for the one imported beer available, Tiger from Singapore. There is surely an opportunity here for someone; wherever tourists go in the East can Heineken be far behind? In Bangkok there are Irish pubs selling Guinness and Caffreys, and last time I was there I walked into a bar to find a full scale promotion for Britain's John Smith's bitter going on. It was double the price of the local *Singha* though.

The river was dark, with only a few lights visible round about us. The stars shone in a clear sky, brilliant pin pricks of light strikingly undiluted by the light pollution we are so often used to in most parts of the world, and the sound of the river was ever present as a kind of living element of the landscape.

Dinner was a real event. A mixture of Asian and Western dishes were served and the sea bass we chose was superb. Needless to say the staff were unstinting and the service was exemplary. Towards the end of the meal a cake was delivered for Lillian. It was her seventieth birthday, and she knew nothing of this, the cake that is, not the birthday, of course. The staff had picked up the fact from her passport details. There were rose petals on the table. There was a special cake and, given where we were, it was as good a place as any to celebrate such an important landmark in one's life.

Privately I hoped that I would still be up to such travelling when I reached a similar age and retired to bed as a precaution to conserve my energy. With more to see before we left Bagan we would have an early start.

*

I am something of a morning person, but the alarm going off at six o'clock felt a bit much on so special a holiday. Still, it made time for a pleasant breakfast ahead of San taking us off for a final tour before the ship set sail at around ten o'clock. Emerging from the cabin we found the morning was magnificent. Everything was still and quiet but there were signs of life too; many people living along the river will get up when it gets light and go to bed when it gets dark. Already along the sandbanks visible in the distance, on which fishermen lived in simple wood and thatch houses, there were signs of activity. Small boats moved along the river border and their silhouettes – the low boat raised at bows and stern and a figure standing to propel the boat forward – were somehow very characteristic of our location. I had made a point of asking and been reassured to hear that there were no crocodiles in the river. Snakes, yes, along the shores, and plenty of fish; these people would come back with a good catch.

After a pleasant breakfast we met San by the gangplank and made the steep climb up path and steps to where the buses waited. In the wet season the river would be much higher and passengers at that time would never see the steps and would be able to walk off to the buses on the level. Marker posts at the top of the slope would, in due course, show the depth of the water alongside the higher shore. Into the English 1 bus it was and we set off into the countryside with San continuing his commentary. He told us only 10 percent of people around spoke any English, and that personal priorities were very clear. "People want a television," he said "then a washing machine and refrigerator, even before a house, then a telephone and car." A car was very much last on the list because, despite the elderly nature of every vehicle around, they were still very expensive. Something from the late eighties could cost US$ 20,000. Many of the few cars we passed were packed with people, and trucks too were loaded to excess, piled precariously high with packages or produce. At one point we also passed a solitary military jeep with two young soldiers in it, the first we had seen. A little later San pointed out fields of castor oil plants or "physics" plants, which were being grown to produce bio-fuel. This was a recent government initiative. They evidently wanted 20 plants planted for every person in the country so that the country would then be self sufficient in fuel. The comparatively small patches we passed, all of which seemed to be struggling, seemed to be unlikely to fuel more than a handful of the generals' personal cars, much less do great things for the economy overall. Fuel availability and cost is a worldwide problem; here, with incomes so low, it must be a particular problem. More so because most of the aged vehicles, struggling along and trailing clouds of fumes, were not doing many miles to the gallon. As food is in short supply too, one might question the priorities here.

We stopped in the bustling main street of a small town and San led us through a narrow passage into the market area. This was open air and what was for sale was mainly food. In such an area, where the arid land would not support much agriculture, most fruit, vegetables and spices came from a distance away; stallholders went to the railway station in the early morning to buy what they would sell during the day and brought it to the market. Stallholder is probably the wrong word, as most "stalls" were no more than a canvas sheet laid out on the ground. Many of the people manning the stalls had what looked like tea towels wrapped round their heads, both as protection from the sun and as a base to steady loads carried on their heads. Business seemed brisk and San assured us everything would be sold out by early afternoon. There were many flowers for sale too, not because people can afford to decorate their homes with them, but because they are believed to keep the business *nats* happy and foster profitable business dealings. So many people buy them for their shop or office. The star shaped *sabai* flower is threaded onto strands of cotton and worn as necklaces or like jewellery.

These decorations are also often hung on shrines and Buddha images as a token of reverence and another way of accruing merit.

Beyond this open section was another area of covered stalls and we were able to wander round real stalls selling a bewildering mixture of things from clothes to household goods. There were also just a few where their wares seemed to be aimed at tourists and that sold handicrafts, amongst which a speciality was grotesque faced puppets in colourful costumes. Some passengers bought things as they went round; indeed shopping seemed a prime motivation for many. Cameras clicked away busily like crickets. I became progressively sure that the couple from Brazil, who were probably in their early thirties, were on honeymoon or had recently got together because he took pictures constantly, but never without taking time for his partner to arrange herself decorously in the foreground of every single shot. Another couple, English Mark and his French wife, who I now realised had not been with us on the bus, then appeared. They had misjudged the departure time and missed the bus. No matter, the powers that be had whistled up a horse and trap for them to catch us up; I half wished it had happened to me as rattling along with a horse in charge seemed a much more exciting mode of transport than the bus.

Nearby was Htilominlo Temple. Built in 1211 it is the last Bamar-style temple built in Bagan, which is about all the guide book says about it, other than that King Nantaungmya ordered it to be built. Well, I suppose kings have to keep themselves busy with something and in Burma if it was not fighting or worrying about being usurped by rivals, then it seems usually to have been erecting some sort of religious building. Reading the history, it often seemed to be all three at once. I have seen no record of how closely such people were involved in this sort of project. Did they just ask for something to be built and leave the rest to the architect or did they supervise the design down to the last tiny detail and check every brick that was laid to make sure it was right? Whichever it was, a common practice was to execute the builder once their work was complete so that they could never better whatever they had built for you. This is one better than the blinding of the architect of the Taj Mahal, which was done for the same reason. You wonder why builders took on such projects; surely they should have preferred to concentrate on houses or something mundane rather than go for the top end of the market when it was likely to be them who would be topped. Perhaps they had no choice; or perhaps the country was full of architects moving to another province just before whatever building they were working on was finished. It would be important to get paid up front too. Anyway, Htilominlo may have rated little detail in the guidebook, but it was a stunning example of its kind. It stood 150 feet high and contained the most common complement of Buddha figures, that is four. Like many temples its decoration includes astrological paintings put there to protect the building from damage. There are, remember, more than 2000 religious buildings in the area. However, given that there were once nearly seven times this number and the rest have either vanished or have left only some minimal ruins, it does not speak highly for the effectiveness of the many protective features they evidently contained. No matter, no one seems to dwell on this and even the most humble dwelling will always have its guardians. It is evidently the kind of belief that demands a healthy measure of optimism alongside it.

The morning's tour was pleasant and interesting and it was all the better for taking place early in the morning before the sun's heat had intensified. But the ship was due to head off for Mandalay at 10a.m. and San hustled us back into the buses and we drove back to meet the deadline. San was immensely knowledgeable. Any question asked of him had him digressing for a moment and giving an answer always replete with precision. Dates and numbers were always exact. He did not have a phrase as stunningly vague as "about twenty" in his lexicon. His enthusiasm was boundless too, and he wanted to see renovation done "right". There was much work being done to preserve the kinds of building we were seeing but some of it was evidently better done than the rest. Above all he wanted us to appreciate his country and the wonders on view. We did.

Back on board the ship we went up to the open top deck to watch the ship get under way.

Chapter Seven

SHIPSHAPE AND SIMPLY GREAT

"The real voyage of discovery consists not
in seeking new landscapes
but in having new eyes."
Marcel Proust

The four thick mooring ropes were released and the ship pulled away from its mooring spot into a river now becoming busier as the day moved into its stride. The river was broad so there was hardly a traffic jam, but other boats were around. Two boats attached to its sides towed a large barge past us. Its cargo consisted of huge logs stacked high. It seemed to be off on a long journey as it had what was clearly living quarters – well, a rough shack - perched precariously on its stern. It indicated a family enterprise, and presumably the kind of family where the kids got taught to swim at an early age. Several small boats were crossing the river on a variety of errands. Even under power and with four engines to drive it along, *Road to Mandalay* was pretty quiet, and any engine noise wafted away to stern. Sitting out on the open deck we watched the journey start. Four members of the crew were visible on the bridge and already, just a few hundred metres from our mooring, the ship was twisting and turning to keep in the main channel and away from any chance of hitting the shifting sand. When the river is low the channel can change within hours as currents shift and care is necessary to make safe passage. Running aground is always a possibility at this time of year. The river has always given cause for concern in this respect. In 1938 a ship equipped with a jet blowing system designed to clear annoying sandbanks was tried. It was no doubt the great hope of its owner that it would work, be in huge demand and make him a fortune. I bet he had a catchy name all ready. *Sands aRen't Us* perhaps. Sadly it rapidly dug itself into a hole and got stuck; such attempts were quickly abandoned, and it seems to have been accepted since that the river has an unchangeable mind of its own. It decides where it will flow, and those using it as a thoroughfare must bend to its wishes.

As the ship pulled away and out into the centre of the river, along the line of the shore the tips of what must have been hundreds of pagodas became visible, and those topped with gold or finished in white, shone brightly in the sunlight. Again the sheer scale of the building in this unique area was made sharply clear. Many of the passengers had opted to sit in the fresh air on the comfortable wicker chairs that furnished the open deck. The swimming pool sparkled in the centre, on the only part of the deck not covered by canvas awnings, but as yet no one had ventured in. Staff members were kept busy delivering drinks, though no one seemed to be taking advantage of the free beer at this still early hour. I did think about it, but I ordered tea, and made a mental note not to forget the beer later on. Imagine a river running through flat countryside without any major features and it might seem to make for a tedious journey. But for us, the reverse proved to be the case.

The scenery was breathtaking, the sky amazing, a huge blue dome above us containing just a few scattered clouds, some white and fluffy, with others less and less distinct trailing away like an aerial splash of milk. Below the sky there was a surprising amount of activity to watch. As the ship adjusted course to follow the channel, guided by a chain of straight branches stuck into the river bed and with maybe three feet of their length sticking out proud of the water, we were first close to one bank and then to the other. Close to shore one could see life going on along the bank. Houses, albeit simple ones, were clustered every so often along both banks, and occasionally these minimal signs of habitation were replaced by the sight of small villages. Then we saw dogs running along the river bank, children waved to us and splashed in the shallows – what about those snakes, I wondered – bullock carts trudged slowly and purposefully along the bank-side paths and left a trail of dust hanging in the still air. There were bicycles and horse drawn carts too, but scarcely anything motorised. People walked along too, singly or in groups, and near the villages we could see some washing either themselves or their clothes in the river, pounding the wet bundles on rocks, and collecting water to take home. Both men and women went into the river wearing their *longyis* to protect their modesty, donning a dry one over the top before divesting themselves of the wet one as they regained the bank.

The land alongside the banks changed as we progressed: first it was totally arid and no more than sand banks, then green and covered in vegetation. Occasionally for no apparent reason a group of boats large enough to be transports of some sort were visible moored by the bank, all alone with no trace of habitation alongside them. I wondered why. Could some of them be pirates ready to board the boats of unwary travellers? No attacks came and it seemed they had no more sinister a purpose than taking a rest. In terms of vessels of any size, the river traffic was sparse, but varied. A two-tier ferry passed us, car tyres hung around its edge as buffers for when it came alongside the shore. There were plenty of people aboard and some of its passengers waved to us. Another boat, a flat ferry of some kind went by going the other way. It was just large enough to carry a dozen cars and trucks on its open deck and was full up. Soon after, a floating petrol station added to the parade. A regular sight continued to be the rafts of logs being floated down river, small thatched huts clinging to the top to house their keepers. People and huts looked rather precariously perched; it is said locally that the most dangerous thing a woman can do is give birth, but for a man it is riding the log rafts.

At one point the channel evidently got particularly difficult to follow. The ship slowed a little, it typically went at between 5 and 8 knots, and the pilot who accompanied the crew on the voyage was called on to supply some high-tech assistance. He and another man left the ship and roared ahead in a large zodiac style rubber dingy with a huge outboard motor at its stern. Hand held radios were produced aboard this and on the ship's bridge. The zodiac proceeded ahead of the ship for a while to show the way. And what high-tech assistance did they supply to fit them for this task? They carried two long, bamboo poles, painted with regular red and white stripes, and pushed them repeatedly into the water, sounding the river to judge its depth. Satisfied by this sight that we were in safe hands, I relaxed still more if such a thing was possible, but my book remained unopened, as there was always something to watch. In what seemed no time the morning was gone and it was time for lunch. We were loath to miss anything, but made our way to the restaurant one deck lower down and sat by one of the large picture windows.

Lunch aboard was a less formal meal than dinner, taken buffet style except for the main course, which arrived consisting of four separate dishes each in one of four bowls set together on one large plate. It was all delightful and so, curious to know who was in charge of all this, I arranged to have a word with the "Hotel Manager": the title chosen presumably to avoid any boat/ship controversy and also any likelihood of someone mistaking them for the captain. Karima Chebanichef may not have skippered the ship, but she was in charge of everything else. She told me she had been doing the job for nearly four years, having previously worked for some of the world's top hotel groups. She must have spent about three weeks with Marriott, Hilton and others she mentioned, as she seemed to me absurdly young for the role. The fact that she was French showed in her, to me, sexy accent and in her stylish appearance. She made making the simplest outfit look a million dollars into an art form − and her figure bore testament to the fact that before going into the hospitality business she had qualified as a dietician. Despite this last, she now spent much of her life ensuring a constant parade of delicious food guaranteed to take the mind of even the most resolute guest off any thoughts of a diet. The gastronomic experience provided on board perhaps confirmed the philosophy of some people that the way to diet is to be on three different diets at once − this being the only way you can get enough to eat. She told me that she had arrived in Burma to start the job with no real knowledge or experience of Asia. "Just one holiday in Thailand when I was quite young," she said. It must have been quite a shock to the culture system, but she must have got to grips with it quickly enough to make a success of the job. Hers must also be a somewhat isolated position. She avoided all comment about how it affected her social life and made no mention of a boy friend. I guess anyone in her life would need extreme patience or a frequent flyer card and an unlimited budget - or all three.

A major part of her job was making sure that the whole team, similarly isolated yet working in the same tight knit group all the time, pulled together and got on well with each other. "Any friction is soon visible to guests," she said. The work schedule was relentless, certainly some staff were up very early so that everything was in order for when their guests rose, and this was no place for anyone inclined to petty jealousies. Staff members were on show and their presence and the service they provided was very much part of the whole experience. My observation showed she was successful in running a tight ship; the staff not only performed well, but also seemed content with their lot and to enjoy the whole business. Given the parlous state of the local economy and low average earnings in the country, they no doubt regarded themselves as lucky to have such jobs, even if they found it difficult to understand us or rather how we could afford such a trip. Well, some of us couldn't really afford it!

Another role she had was to ensure good relations with the communities the ship passed through along the river. For example, she and the ship's doctor were involved in charity work to help people in various villages, for instance providing help with schools, especially at nursery level. They contributed in a tangible and practical way, "If we simply gave money," she said, "it might be diverted." She didn't elaborate, but went on, "What we do helps mothers who otherwise could not work and thus boosts family income as well as education." Education is just one of the things that is inadequate in Burma and in most parts of the country you are more likely to see pupils working with a slate and chalk rather than on a computer. Ironically, some of the few schools that do have a computer have no electricity. Poor education has knock on effects too and helps keep people in poverty. I was told that families are keen for their children to learn, but that it is typical for a child to go to school only for a short time, then having to leave and go to work so that a younger sibling can then use the limited resources available for education. In this way at least most children do learn some basics, such as reading and writing.

Only a minor part of Karima's job seemed to involve any major problem. If the ship ran aground, something that has been known to happen occasionally when the river is low, then the captain and his crew sorted that out. Passengers sometimes presented with minor problems: people regularly came back from a visit to a pagoda or religious site, where they had to take their shoes off to go inside, wearing someone else's footwear. A better or worse pair, I wonder? Another complaint that occurred was that people reported that the television in their cabin had been stolen. In such cases Karima had simply to point out diplomatically that the unit housing the television was controlled by a button alongside the bed: press this and the television sinks down inside the unit to provide more space in the cabin. Any "stolen" ones thus magically reappeared at the touch of a button.

Soon Karima was to swap this exclusive, but enclosed, world for a new job in a resort hotel in Laos. As I was sure that anywhere in which she had a hand was likely to be good, I made a note of the name: it is called La Residence Phou Vao in case you want a classy holiday in Laos. Because of this impending move, on this particular voyage her successor was on board learning the ropes. Esther Siemoneit was another attractive young women – I wonder if this tells us anything about the Human Resources manager responsible for recruitment in this company, I had met two of their staff in London – Anna and Louise - and they were also both attractive young women. Karima's successor was in the same mould: in this case a blonde German who would take over in similar circumstances. That is, despite a successful career in hospitality she had, as yet, no knowledge of Asia. The words deep and end came to mind, but she professed herself unfazed by it all. The company seemed to have a strange specification for such a job, it seemed that candidates must be young, attractive and female, speak several languages and be happy to be away from home for months at a time. Oh, and having no knowledge or experience at all of Asia seemed to help. Despite all this she gave me no reason to doubt that she would prove as competent as the current incumbent clearly is.

While in the mood to check things out I also got myself an invitation to visit the bridge. The captain, helmsman and the two Rivermasters, who had earlier been leading the way in their dinghy, sat in a row. The captain, Myo Lwin, was identifiable from his uniform. Even though he wore casual trousers and a simple a white shirt, the gold braiding on his shoulders was unmistakable. A naval looking peaked cap sat against the forward window in front of him. Until recently he had been a merchant navy man, but now wanting to spend more time with his family he had turned to something smaller and nearer to home. He commanded the largest vessel on the entire river. Size does count for something and as he said, "most other boats get out of our way". He admitted that the river could be tricky, particularly at this time of year when the dry season makes it so shallow. "You have to take care," he said, "here still waters may well run shallow, the signs can be confusing and the channel is only as wide as we are in some places, even where the river itself is very wide. Rocks are the real problem, most of the river is sand and if we hit that occasionally – no problem, but we do need to avoid the rocks." Yes, please - we had already seen some largish vessels marooned and heard tales of some that had been stuck for months. He pointed to a spot on the water off to port, saying, "Rocks there". It seemed no different to me than any other swirl of water. He explained that signs erected on the bank helped to mark the channel, as did the markers, sticks actually, set along the river in the channel itself. Another important sign was a red flag on the bank indicating that the ship should not make excessive waves that might hurt some sensitive village activity. I asked him about the equipment on the ship. The bridge was ablaze with illuminated dials and a variety of, mostly red, lights. He was happy to explain, saying that they had both modern sonar and radar. "The sonar is no help, no good, it doesn't work," he said without hint of apology, "and the radar is useless, its signal just bounces off the banks. I only switch it on so that the lights show and impress the passengers. It is the people who matter, I watch his face" – he peered over his spectacles and indicated one of the Rivermasters – "that tells me more than all the electronics. It certainly tells me if we are in trouble." He laughed and I wondered how much of what he said was true. One way or another, everything was doubtless under control. Only some random factor that registered on neither equipment nor face could spoil our safe passage, and for all I know there was a *nat* aboard somewhere for just such an emergency.

When I asked his permission, he let me take the wheel for a few minutes. Unfortunately it was at a time when to follow the channel the ship had to zigzag and head for a sign on the starboard shore. It thus looked as if I was steering the ship off course and straight into the bank. Some of the other passengers noticed and, despite my explanations, and my turning to port in due course exactly as directed, some people seemed to lack faith in my abilities. One of the German passengers joined us on the bridge. She had links with the world of engineering, had been doing some checking of her own and had discovered that, like the ship itself, the four engines were also German built. This she adamantly claimed was the most important thing in guaranteeing our safety; such a triumph of engineering would not let us down she insisted. To make her point she added, "This is well known, don't you have a German car?" I confessed not, and avoided a debate about the relative merits of Mercedes, Audi and BMW, and Volvo, only by pointing out something on the shore. I'm sure the ship's German engines constituted an undeniable asset. Indeed they may well have been crucial to keeping it operating properly and preventing it deteriorating into an eastern version of *The African Queen*. If I had inadvertently steered the ship into the bank, something that was never in prospect mark you, then we had the certainty of German excellence to save the day and pull us off again. Personally I found both my steering and the knowledge that the engines were sound reassuring. This feeling was diluted a little later on. I noticed that the life rafts, which were stowed in cylinder like containers along the edge of the deck, and some of which I passed on leaving the bridge, were also German made. But they had notices on them indicating that they were due for a service in only a couple of months. I would have preferred to be sailing just after a successful service rather than just before one was due. The captain had praised the engines, but also said that the engineer in charge of them was "... kept in the stern where I can't see his face". I hoped that there were more ways of reporting any difficulty with the engines than a troubled look. People and engines seemed to perform flawlessly during our whole trip, but I still felt it had been a good idea to get the nod from the captain himself. Despite his jocular manner and disparaging remarks about the electronic equipment, he cut a confident figure and I felt we were safe in his hands. Later Karima told me that the captain had never let any other passenger steer in the past. She looked puzzled. Perhaps she was not thinking that my obvious confidence and expertise made me a worthy exception. I imagined her tackling him later and saying: "Are you mad? Never do that again!" Maybe though the captain was not losing his mind, perhaps no one else had ever asked, or at least not asked and coupled it with a promise to immortalise him in print; maybe even captains can be a little vain.

Today we would cruise all day, mooring at dusk at some point in mid river to be safe overnight from pirates, wild animals, snakes and any other potential dangers. First there was more to keep us busy. During the afternoon we had a demonstration of how to tie a *langyi* in preparation for a *langyi* cocktail party in the evening. Men tie this traditional garment in front, while women tie theirs at the side tucking the knot into a waistband. These really are all purpose garments. They can be simple or formal, worn with a shirt or blouse or with a more formal matching top. San, for instance, wore his with a white shirt and a smart black collarless jacket. Tying them was more complicated than it appeared. The instructions began: step in, spread out the *longyi* panel of cloth and wrap the excess cloth around the waist from front to side. But later instructions advised the use of safety pins and this no doubt makes it easier. Some of the passengers were successfully dressed in this way, and even some of the men looked well - let's say rather fetching. Me? Once I had it on, I divested myself of it again in moments. The other demonstration carried out as this went on was to give people a chance to appreciate the traditional *thanaka*. This is a powder traditionally used by women and children on their cheeks and sometimes on other exposed skin. It comes from grinding bark mixed with a little water to make a paste and is said to give protection from the sun as well as softening and lightening the skin. Acting as a sunscreen and beauty aid combined, people buy it, not in a pot, but in the form of a small log. These usually come from the north of the country and they provide the raw material from which the *thanaka* can be made. So if you see what looks like a stall selling firewood in a market here, then it is likely the local equivalent of The Body Shop. Quite a number of the women passengers tried this, and had it applied to their cheeks in a way that left leaf shaped impressions. One or two were still sporting the adornment in the evening; though whether they were just entering into the spirit of things, or desperately hoping that it really would have a rejuvenating effect on their skin I do not know.

The afternoon went peacefully by, and the river never lost its mesmerising effect. The time seemed to speed up and, before we knew it, the boat slowed and, as planned, dropped anchor on a wide and peaceful stretch of river half an hour or so before sunset. All was still and quiet round about us. Few lights were visible as dusk descended and soon it was time to get ready for dinner. There was the "*langyi* cocktail party" on the upper deck scheduled ahead of the meal and what was described enigmatically by the crew as "a surprise" to come later in the evening. People guessed at what that might be. Most favoured fireworks, but somehow this seemed less eco-friendly than our unspoilt surroundings deserved, so it failed to get my vote. Besides in so quiet a setting I could not believe that the noise of fireworks would make them a likely choice. I thought maybe they would launch small hot air balloons of the sort favoured in Thailand as part of a firework display, especially at New Year when they are believed to float away past sins, but this suffered from the same problem. We were all proved wrong and later the event was a genuine surprise to everyone.

I had resolved to make this trip in style and so far everything fitted the bill well; it was all immensely civilised. As is the way when a group of strangers meet, we discovered at the cocktail party that the only other English person on board, Mark, travelling with his French wife Nicholle, lived very near my sister-in-law in Cambridgeshire. Such coincidences are surprisingly common. On the now softly lit upper deck drinks were served and I had one more free beer. I continued to think that this was a splendid idea. If you run a hotel, restaurant or similar do *please* feel free to copy it, especially if yours is a business I can frequent. Meanwhile, around me wine glasses were topped up on a regular basis. We chatted to Lillian and Sandy, the American ladies who were finishing a trip that had started in Vietnam. Sandy's late husband had served there and she had particularly wanted to visit, though the experience had not been the satisfying one she hoped for with demons being put satisfactorily to rest. She had found it a mixed experience, and in some ways it seemed to have been upsetting. Nevertheless she was enjoying the warm evening air and allowed her generously proportioned wine glass to be topped up several times. In fact, by the end of dinner, during which she ordered more wine, she was a little the worse for wear and departed early to her cabin, missed the surprise and was cross with herself about it the following day. Although the gathering was billed as *longyi* cocktails, few passengers appeared so clad and none who did wore them on into dinner.

Dinner was again a delightful experience. The food on the ship was a mixture of western and Asian dishes. Everything was presented with great style and attention to detail. I heard no complaints, and indeed people commented on the level of gastronomic delight. Then, at about 9-30 p.m., passengers were invited to return to the upper deck. Once there, most of the lights on deck were extinguished and we were still unsure what was coming. As our eyes became accustomed to the dark we saw a long line of light ahead of us up the river. Gradually the light resolved itself into many individual lights apparently floating towards us on the current. There were literally hundreds and hundreds of them and, as they spread out and drifted nearer, we could see that they were in fact candles each sitting on its own tiny raft. The effect was simply magical. The river and its surrounds were quiet. Apart from the multitude of stars in the sky there were no lights to speak of around and this amazing spectacle lit up the river. By the time they came close to the ship they were well spread out and passed on both sides, moving silently on into the distance to stern and disappearing around a bend in the river. It was sheer magic, heightened by the silence and the setting and it far outdid the earlier thoughts of fireworks. How was this spectacle possible?

The ship had not, in fact, moored at random as it had appeared to do earlier in the evening. Rather it had been carefully positioned so that a group of the crew, assisted by a team of people recruited from a nearby village, could set up this convoy of light and send it on its way. They had done so working from a small fleet of boats, while they had remained invisible in the darkness. The flotilla of candle lights themselves – there were 2007 of them to mark the date – were small candles housed on little rafts made of bamboo leaves. So many: no wonder they gave such a dramatic show. They were carefully constructed to be biodegradable too; even so a collection party of crewmen would go out soon after dawn to collect as many as possible from the sandbank that normally caught them before we sailed on. All this must have taken some organising, but it was some spectacle.

It made a perfect end to a wonderful day, and we retired to our cabin contented.

Chapter Seven

Chapter Eight

WHERE THE
FLYING FISHES PLAY

*"My favourite thing is to go where
I have never gone."*
Diane Arbus

Morning: the zodiac dinghy was out maybe a hundred metres in front of us again, the red and white poles plunging and rising in high-tech unison to ensure our safe passage. This was, as the captain had put it a "channel as wide as ship" stretch. The river itself was now broad; though we had just come through a narrow channel with high banks, made a tight ninety degree turn and were now proceeding in a zigzag fashion in the wake of the dinghy. Long low sand bars fronted the river banks on either side and some other stretches of shore looked like the salt marshes near my English home on an East coast estuary: the water was mostly inundating areas of green vegetation and long channels were visible disappearing into its depths. There seemed to be fewer birds about than one would expect in such unspoilt countryside, but here there were numbers of heron-like wading birds along the water's edge. They presumably had their own territory and could make a good living from the river, but as I watched two clashed and went for the same fish and the whole group became rambunctious for a few moments. They stood again with regal stature and every so often one of them lunged into the water after something tasty. A fish would need a measure of good luck to escape these precision strikes.

If they inhabited the same spot regularly, then local people might get to know particular birds. Two brightly coloured ducks often visit the estuary outside my house, seemingly waddling about like an old married couple. Our neighbours have christened them Howard and Hilda after characters in the television sit-com, *Ever Decreasing Circles*: a husband and wife who always appeared wearing identical clothes, usually topped by brightly patterned pullovers. Here there was no sign of habitation, people or other river traffic, and no one to christen any particularly distinctive bird.

Told by the captain that we would be traversing the most difficult stretch of river on our journey early in the morning, I had got up early and was sitting at a bar stool at the stern end of the open top deck before 7 a.m. I watched our passage through all this in comfort with a cup of tea poured by Lwin Soe, who told me that he had to rise at 5.30 a.m. "... to get new uniform, and everything ready for you". I think he meant everyone rather than just me. His fresh white shirt was spotless, despite the work he was doing to get the serving area ready for its day's business, his blue striped *longyi* was neatly tied and he had paused briefly from his polishing to make me a cup of tea. The bar was spotless. He worked with a fervour that suggested he had a conviction that the entire voyage would be in jeopardy if his particular tasks were not executed to perfection. It reflected the way in which every member of the crew went about their work. The sun shone and was still sufficiently low in the sky at this time of the morning that it made a wonderful long band of reflected gold and red colours, which stretched across the sparkling water.

The deck was virtually empty. The only other people in evidence were Lillian, minus her companion who was having a little difficulty getting to grips with the day and regretting the excess of wine the previous evening and her subsequent missing of the night's surprise candle-lit spectacular. With Lillian was Sue, half of the New York couple living in Hong Kong. These two chatted quietly over their cups of tea or coffee. Sue was with a large American bank, and probably led the pressurised life of such a person, so this was, I hoped, allowing her to wind down satisfactorily. Indeed, I reckoned that if she, or anyone else for that matter, could not relax in this environment, she should give up and consider a radical career change.

The river currently showed some rough patches almost like small rapids, though no rocks were actually visible above the surface. The zodiac stayed on station for more than an hour. The red and black poles plunged ceaselessly in and out of the water, and I remembered from the previous day that the captain had told me that often the river was as little as seven feet deep at this time of year: "No matter, this gives us two feet in hand. And two inches would do," he said. He should know, but it seemed a minuscule margin and I imagined the fish running for cover as the ship's bottom loomed over them. The view changed as we went further on; first there were small houses visible on the bank, then a village and shortly after that what appeared to be a small town with a road running for a while alongside the stream. Motorbikes and other vehicles were both visible and audible as we came closer to the bank, and we drew quite close to a ferry, a vessel about half our length. As we did so, both captains sounded a "good morning" blast on their hooters as they drew parallel to each other and as the *Road to Mandalay* overtook.

This sort of trip, at least in its quieter moments, seems to be one long round of consumption. Tea on deck, breakfast and then tea on deck again, this time with a minor language problem: ordering tea I thought the waitress had asked, "What make?" It seemed a rather odd question, but I replied naming the brand they usually seemed to serve, "Tetley, please." This reply produced great puzzlement until I discovered that what she had actually said was, "With milk?" A "Yes, please" got us safely back on track, her puzzled look disappeared and her smile returned. Despite the fact that most passengers seemed both happy and to find the constantly changing view fascinating, the management did not intend that a single moment should be allowed to become boring and arranged various diversions like the *langyi* wearing instruction course of yesterday. With a clear morning ahead as we went up river, and with no stops or excursions, there had to be another such event.

And this morning it was to be me.

Having discovered that I had written a book[1] about travelling in the region, I had been recruited to talk about it. Not, I have to say, because of my fame, but because I was there. I was a cheap option, indeed a free one. Notices had gone up in various places on board and, in due course, an announcement was made over the loud speakers and soon after I found myself sitting on a stool in the Piano Bar in front of a goodly proportion of the passengers. Karima had

---

[1] *First Class At Last!* by Patrick Forsyth, Rethink Press.

doubtless selected this venue so that if people became bored they could at least have a stiff drink and nibble some nuts to take their minds off it. I told myself that only those lacking fluency in English had stayed away. Most authors respond positively to any opportunity to plug a book. This is no surprise because the only thing more difficult than getting published (it is estimated that publishers get more than 2,000 ideas and manuscripts for every one that they actually turn into a book) is getting attention focused on a book once it has been published. Besides publishers encourage authors to do this and claim that talking about a book is somehow respectable. No one would be likely to ask Sue, say, to give a talk about her bank, even less to describe why we should favour it by opening an account at it. This would be rampant commercialism. But an author talking about their writing, and in this case also about travelling, and reading some extracts from their tome is considered okay. This is despite the fact that it is done primarily to create visibility and sell copies. In my case I was still getting used to this sort of thing. I had done a short signing session in the only bookshop in the small town where I live just before flying out here. I had not had to say anything formal then, just smile gratefully and express appreciation when anyone came in and bought a copy, which amazingly some people did. I even had one famous visitor. A well-known and successful novelist came, Neal Asher who lives locally and is known for his science fiction (start with *Gridlinked* if you like that sort of thing). He not only bought a copy, but also wrote about it later in the blog attached to his web site and sent his personal recommendation winging its way through the ether. This time I had to give a talk. After the announcement people came on time and appeared to find such an event acceptable.

Just after the appointed hour, Karima stood up, the chatter died down and I was introduced. My wife had been very stern with me about one aspect of this. Despite the fact that, in accepting the invitation, I had made a point of asking how long my session should last, she told me to be very careful and, "not to go on for too long". She did not define "too long", but I seem to remember that she mentioned it more than once in a tone of voice that reminded me of a couple we had seen being photographed a while back. The photographer had asked, "And now one with your wife?" and she had replied, "I'm not his wife, I'm his boss." My wife's comment was not said in such a way, of course, but there are still certain tones of voice that signal that any argument is fruitless. So, I began my talk by quoting A.A. Milne. He was, of course, the author of the Winnie the Pooh books, which are probably part of almost every English person's childhood, and was a well-known literary figure in his day. Asked to attend the launch party held for another author's book, he did so but, when someone asked him afterwards how it had been, he is reputed to have replied, "It took him three quarters of an hour to tell us how he came to write the wretched book, when all we needed was an apology."

Quoting this drew smiles and acted also to remind me that my wife is usually (always?) right about such things. I promised not to keep people too long, kept an eye on the time, spoke a little about writing and getting the book published, about the journey involved, read a couple of extracts and finished with what I thought was admirable precision, one minute inside my allotted half hour. At the end almost all the English speakers bought a copy of the book. I had optimistically carried a bundle of them half way across the world for just such a possibility; please note my zeal, Mr Publisher. I duly signed most of them too, on request. I am still very much at the stage of waiting to be asked to sign a book. It seems pretentious to do so unasked, just assuming that people want you to do so. What is more, I fear doing so unasked may be seen as attempting to lay claim to a level of literary fame, which in my case is certainly premature. In any case my morning diversion seemed to have passed satisfactorily, no one fell asleep or walked out and there were smiles and laughter where I hoped there would be. At the end Karima, who had attended with a few of her colleagues from the staff, thanked me for my efforts. As the gathering broke up several guests took photographs. Some people will photograph anything; for a moment I wondered if it was too late to negotiate terms for film rights.

Afterwards, back on the top deck, Lillian arrived wearing a swimming costume ready to try out the ship's pool. She chose a chair, dropped her bag and towel and approached not the pool but me. "If you are planning to write about this trip, I suppose you will want some real incidents along the way – what can I do, drown?" She had been at my talk, indeed both she and Sandy, who was back to her perky self, had purchased books. She smiled as I assured her nothing so drastic was necessary. I can only report that she swam calmly up and down for a while, pronounced it very pleasant and did not make more than a ripple as she did so; elegant, but certainly not dramatic.

We had lunch to go before we moored at Shwe Kyat Yet, a small village constituting the ship's base close to Mandalay;

the captain promised he would juggle with his speed to ensure we arrived after lunch so that, "I do not spoil your meal. Once there you will all want to go and explore." Miss lunch? Perish the thought. Twelve kitchen staff, working under head chef Yannis Martineau, ensure that meals on board are very much part of what makes a voyage on the *Road to Mandalay* so special. Apart from one Frenchman in the kitchen all these people are Burmese, as are the twenty waiters and waitresses. Yannis likes to be in touch with his guests and is often in personal attendance during buffet style meals, explaining to the gastronomically challenged like me just exactly what everything is and, should you be interested, how it is made. Much of the food, fruit and vegetables and so on, are bought in Burma. Other specialist items are sourced from wherever is necessary to ensure the best: smoked salmon comes from Scotland, cheese is from Normandy and strawberries come from Australia. Supplies are assembled in Singapore and a forty-foot sea-container is used to bring everything to Yangon. It must be a logistical nightmare, but is clearly made to work well and there was no evidence of anything running out unexpectedly during the voyage. Meanwhile, outside the scenery changed again, more signs of habitation were in evidence, and by the dessert stage of the meal the mountains that rise above Mandalay were visible in the distance.

There was time for people to comfortably finish lunch and be out on deck to watch proceedings as the ship sailed towards Mandalay. Before we reached the mooring, there were two bridges to negotiate. For a long time there have been only two bridges on the river's entire two thousand-plus kilometres: one at Pyay and one, the Ava or Inwa Bridge, built by the British in 1934. Even if some would say that we don't make the best engines in the World, and that could be contested, bridges we like to think we do know about, and the German engineering lady admitted to knowing of Brunel. She even managed to allow a hint of respect to sound in the comment.

The bridge was destroyed in World War II by the British to hold up the Japanese advance in 1942, and was only rebuilt in 1954. Its 16 steel spans carry both road and rail traffic, with the railway line going to Myitkyina. Having said the river boasts only two bridges, a third one is going up here right alongside the steel hoops and concrete of the current one. The new one, not quite finished as we passed it, will take the road traffic, leaving the old bridge with just the railway to carry. The new one is needed to link to new roads, and a highway to India, and because the old bridge can no longer take the weight of traffic now put on it; already heavy vehicles are diverted and must take one of the ferries. Having seen the reckless way in which some trucks and buses here are loaded, it is difficult to imagine any bridge that could safely take them. No doubt the new bridge will help matters, and the extraordinary small number of bridges along such a stretch of river certainly explains the number of boats and ferries criss-crossing the river all along its length.

A number of passengers clustered around the bridge, the ship's bridge that is, as we approached these bridges. The captain, who presumably would get a break when we stopped here, was in a merry mood. He announced that we should all exercise great care as, "The bridge is very low, best you all sit down as we go under." He also more sensibly recommended that we cover our ears as four shatteringly loud ten-second blasts on the ship's hooter announced our arrival to the surrounding populace. The ship slowed, passed under both the old and new bridge and turned to starboard to make its way towards its designated mooring. At the top of the beach were rudimentary buildings, many with thatched roofs, their frontages giving evidence of their purpose with piles of bulging sacks or visible goods. As we approached the bank, the four engines were used in turn and combination to fit us neatly into just the right mooring spot.

A large red and gold sign at the top of the bank marked the *Road to Mandalay's* base on a very busy section of river bank. Either side, the shore at the edge of the long sloping bank housed dozens of boats of all sizes; some were tied one to another with the furthest offshore needing people to climb over the others to access them. A variety of rickety looking gangways led across from boat to boat and boat to shore giving access to higher sections of the bank. Goods of all sorts were being loaded and unloaded and loudspeakers added their noise to the general hubbub. San told us that the voices were calling out to link particular pieces of cargo and their owners: "Your new outboard motor is here Mr. Sei, come and collect it quickly." It must be fun when certain goods are ordered and the whole community is told that your consignment of pile ointment or something more embarrassing is being brought ashore. Thin lines were tossed ashore from *Road to Mandalay*, quickly caught by helpers ashore and used to pull the heavy mooring ropes across and make us secure amid this scene. It was all slickly done and, although he must have done it many times before, the helmsman could rightly be pleased with himself for achieving it with such precision. The way he gently nudged the bank made the landing our Air Mandalay pilot had subjected us to a few days back seem like the work of a Kamikaze pilot failing by a narrow margin.

This was it. I had set my heart on seeing Mandalay and now I would. It is a young city, founded only in 1857 and became the capital in 1861 when King Mindon, who may be the only one of Burma's seemingly numberless monarchs to have a pronounceable name, moved in with 150,000 people and his entire palace entourage. He built a magnificent Royal Palace at the foot of Mandalay Hill and established the "Golden City" foreseen by an ancient Buddhist prophecy stemming from a time when the Buddha himself is reputed to have climbed the hill. King Mindon had his bad side: for instance he killed and buried 52 men and women in strategic locations around the palace so that their spirits would act as guards and protect the palace forever. It seems an odd way to go about things. Apart from anything else what possible grounds could he have had for thinking that spirits so created would buckle down and help the person who had had them so brutally killed? If spirits can be miffed, then these surely would have been miffed in a very big way. His successor, the slightly more impenetrably named King Thibaw, also excelled in the tyrant department. In fact he engaged in such excesses, killing large numbers of his subjects and foreigners alike, that he prompted the invasion by the British in 1885. After that, in 1886, Yangon became the capital and remained so during the colonial period. Mandalay was then a far flung outpost of the British Empire, Burma being run as a kind of satellite of the major British outpost, India. The original palace was huge: the wall surrounding it was almost two kilometres long and a moat added protection outside that. The palace itself was exquisitely carved in wood, and was surrounded by temples and monasteries. It was destroyed by shellfire in 1945 as the British tried to dislodge occupying Japanese soldiers. Although some renovation has been done, the grounds within the moat are now shared by Mandalay Fort and are occupied by the army. The shores of the moat itself, which is 75 yards wide and some ten feet deep, is a popular place for a stroll and a picnic. As well it might be as it was recently cleared and put back in order by what the government call donated labour, saying people are happy to earn merit this way by completing so worthy a task. Donated labour is what many other people call forced labour, and you would be hard pressed to find anyone with a good word to say about it.

No longer the capital (the designation of which town is currently the Burmese capital moves about like unpredictable jumping frogs), Mandalay remains an impressive town, not least because the hill above it, covered to its summit with temples and pagodas, is impressive and affords, as we would see later, a spectacular view from the top.

It was time for another tour and San was back to organise it. As we left the ship to get on another bus, still bearing the English 1 sign, the passengers snaked across one gangway onto shore, while another at the stern had a line of people going the other way carrying supplies on and into the bowels of the ship. "It always seems like a line of ants," said Karima who was at the entrance to see her charges on their way. Everything that must be taken on board, everything presumably except water and fuel, which is piped on, must be packed in individual people-can-carry-quantities and physically brought on board in this way. The ants were probably going to be moving to and fro for a while.

Though the ship was to be our hotel, as it were, while we saw something of Mandalay, the voyage along the river was over. We had travelled nearly 200 kilometres since boarding the boat and every single one of them had been pleasurable. While the scenery, and the life of people along the way, had been fascinating to observe, the river was not, of course, primarily there for our pleasure. It has always acted as a national highway of the country and a lifeline for its people. Today it was busy too, a real working river. We had shared it with a profusion of different craft: bamboo rafts, fishing boats large and small, ferries, some of them double-deckers, and a host of other vessels whose specific purpose was not obvious. In some ways this is a minor amount of traffic compared with its heyday. From the mid-nineteenth century through to 1942, the Irrawaddy Flotilla Company ruled the river. This Glasgow-based company began operations with four steamers and three cargo boats, but by 1930 there were 602 vessels and they carried nine million people every year. Colonialism may have a good deal to answer for in some respects, but my goodness it seems to have bred a unique brand of entrepreneurial spirit. We are used to what is called the global village these days, but it must have taken a peculiar vision to sit in Victorian Glasgow and say, "You know, I think putting a few hundred boats on that river out in Burma might make us a bob or two." In its time it was rightly called the greatest river fleet on Earth. Like so much else it became a victim of war. In 1942, as the Japanese invaded, its then manager John Morton had the entire fleet scuttled to prevent the enemy from enlisting it for the Japanese war effort. Nearly one hundred of these ships still lie mouldering below the river's surface today; their hulls still full of the bullet holes inflicted to sink them. The company began to revive after the war, but was then nationalised; the remnants now operate as the Government Inland Water Transport Board. One small link to the past is provided by the continuing use of the old colours, and all the funnels of present day ships are painted red and black.

The pace of life along the river is slow. On the river nothing moves at more than a few knots and large loads on barges can take a month or more to run down to the delta, hence the shacks on board to provide accommodation. Some 75% of Burma's population live in rural areas, many of them along the river, leading simple lives that have not changed essentially for centuries; and most are affected not at all by tourism. By contrast present day Mandalay is a bustling town of two million people and I was thrilled to be able to explore it. We settled onto the bus and it pulled away trailing a swirling cloud of red-ochre dust.

Chapter Nine

ON THE TOWN

"Certainly, travel is more than seeing the sights;
it is a change that goes on, deep and
permanent in the ideas of living."
Miriam Beard

We overtook a Tourismo Asia van full of westerners, in what might almost have been a show of superiority by our driver, and the red dust we were kicking up quickly obscured them to our rear. Then we slowed again, as in front of us was a local bus. Battered looking and bouncing over the rough road, its roof was piled high with packages of all shapes and sizes to a level that almost doubled its height. Mandalay is sometimes referred to as the "city of bikes" and plenty of those were piled on top too, ready to take their owners onwards when their journey left the bus route. There seemed to be more people clinging to the outside of the bus than there were in its interior. San assured us that the conductor, clinging on there somewhere, would only charge half price when the bus was so full that someone could only hold on with one hand rather than two. This sounded fair but, even in a place of such different mores, I was not sure whether to take him literally.

We turned off the main road as we went towards the town and stopped at a stone-carving workshop. The showroom, actually a courtyard in front of the wooden building, was full of Buddha images: some seated, some standing, some reclining. Some were tabletop size, but others towered over us. A few other figures were mixed in and, of course, Lillian wanted to know if any of them were *nats*. Indeed, some were, so we should be safe during our visit, though what power a half carved *nat* has is likely to be even more uncertain than that for a complete one. Still, in a troubled world, I guess if they kept people even half safe that was better than nothing. Like so many crafts, and certainly many such things we saw here, it is easy to look at a finished product and underestimate what is involved in producing it. There were figures here at every stage of carving; big stones just beginning to turn into figures, clear but unfinished figures and faces, and some just needing a final polish. Marble chips covered the floor and dust covered absolutely everything. Women always did the polishing, San told us, because, "They are more patient". A number of female faces around him twitched slightly. Right, I thought, and they are doubtless lower paid and inclined to do as they are told here. Whatever the reason, they made an excellent job of it. The polishing is done using stones, with seven different levels of roughness being used in turn to get to the final marble-smooth finish.

The local market for this kind of thing must be huge, and in addition many were being made for export, often to China and Thailand. A large figure might be sold for US$4,000, a sum which, given the average wage, said something about how long they took to make. I can never look at something like this without wondering about the failure rate. How often, I wonder, does a figure go through weeks of work, get within a chip or two of being finished and then have say, a finger or a nose inadvertently hacked off by mistake? And what happens then? Perhaps they reuse it, cutting into the exposed full features and reducing it to a smaller scale. Maybe the smaller figures ranged around us were evidence of poor workmanship. Or maybe they are just sold at a discount: ten percent off for one with one ear missing and fifteen percent off for one with no nose. In fact, the considerable skill employed by the sculptors was obvious and the entire set up was one vast apprenticeship scheme too: newcomers only carved the rough shape, gradually adding to their repertoire as they gained more skill, while the best and most experienced craftsmen did the detailed work. The real dunces presumably spent a lifetime hewing rough outlines or moved on to some other occupation.

Not only did this workshop represent quite an operation, quite an industry, it was not alone – the entire street was inhabited by stone carvers and there must have been forty or fifty workshops strung along the road with presumably people buying from the one their grandfather had used as they did at the shops in Yangon. After a good look round, and when even the most dedicated shoppers in the group had failed to buy a six foot stone figure to tuck under their arm and tax their packing and baggage allowance still more, we moved on.

Gold is a dominant colour in many temples and similar structures and what makes this so in many cases is, well... gold. Women sometimes say it is not possible to be too thin. Well, gold leaf is almost unbelievably thin. Gold leaf brings a whole new meaning to the word thin; touch a small piece just an inch or so square and it curls onto your finger. Try to move it and it breaks into tiny pieces, each with an almost sticky texture. Adding gold leaf to a religious statue of some sort, most usually a Buddha image, is an act of reverence. It pays homage to the figure and the whole lifestyle it represents. This act is an inherent part of Burmese life, so naturally San arranged for us to have a go and that meant we visited yet another pagoda.

Maha Muni Pagoda is probably the most important religious structure in Mandalay, so much so that it is simply known as the "Great Pagoda". A king called Bodawpaya built it in 1784, though what you see today dates from a rebuilding after a fire a hundred years or so later. Its central image, a Buddha figure stolen from the Arakanese to the West of the country by the King's troops, attracts pilgrims from far and wide. Its age is uncertain, but put at around AD 146. Legend says that Sakka, king of the gods, created it as a likeness of Gautama Buddha: its likeness being so lifelike that only a heavenly being could have created it. However it originated, it is a survivor. It has been lost and found, captured and moved around, broken into three pieces and reassembled, and still remains impressive. Cast in metal, it stands nearly four metres high and is now coated in gold leaf several centimetres thick over most of its surface. Even so, this is clearly universally regarded as sadly inadequate, because when we got there the figure sat in an array of scaffolding used to support steps up and around it, and a constant line of people filed past, each to stick just a little more gold onto the figure. I presume the steps are moved on a regular basis otherwise one portion of the figure's anatomy would bulge disproportionately. Today was small of the back day and we were invited to get in line, climb up and add our small contribution. How many travel companies throw in a little gold with the price of the trip? With some it is difficult to get them to include a sandwich to keep body and soul together on the flight. On such a trip as this it was no problem and San handed out a small piece of gold leaf to us all.

When I say "us all" I mean the men in the party. The figure is off limits to women, as indeed are many other religious images. Why? Well, of course San could supply the reason. It hinged on what may well have been the first recorded case of celebrity stalking. Legend has it that many years ago a woman took to following Buddha and particularly to following him when he retired home to sleep at night. She succeeded in doing this in a way that created rumours that they were, how shall we say, intimately acquainted – this being something that was not regarded as very Buddha-like behaviour. Having started the rumours she appeared one day apparently visibly pregnant and the rumours shot up a notch or two on the scandal scale. It turned out that it was all a trick, a cushion was discovered beneath her clothes and the honour of the Buddha was restored. Since then women have been restricted in certain ways within many religious places, presumably in case any others should dream up some new and inappropriate trickery. Here there was a kind of holding area, to which the women in our party were directed, while us more politically correct men went to add our gold. One thing made me wonder if I really understood the significance and reverence of all this. As I made my way in line towards and up the steps, the mobile phone of the Burmese man in front of me rang. He then conducted a loud conversation that went on all the way up and all the way down and he did not even pause while he added his gold leaf. What was so important I wonder that he could not put it off for a moment? Maybe he was explaining to his wife that far from wasting his time and money in the pub, he was engaged in a more worthy pursuit and would be home soon. Maybe his conversation included saying, "I'm at the temple", in the same way that carriages in Britain's railways echo with innumerable mobile users using the ubiquitous and fellow-passenger-annoying phrase, "I'm on the train". Already my small addition must be buried under the numerous layers that must have been added since, but it is there somewhere and likely to remain so for many years given this figure's importance and exceptional record of survival. I like the thought of that.

The women were allowed to see and touch at our next port of call. Outside in one of the courtyard areas of Maha Muni are six ancient Kymer bronze statues. Originally amongst the guardians of Cambodia's immense Angkor Wat, a place so famous that it is now overrun with tourists, they were stolen during a Thai raid in 1431 and taken to Ayutthaya, the ancient Thai capital. They then embarked on some significant travels. In 1564 they were stolen again and taken to Bago after the sacking of Ayutthaya by King Bayinnaung, and in 1600 they were moved to Mrauk-U. They have had a more settled existence since 1784 in their current home. A few were lost along the way - what a surprise - and the six that survive and are displayed here are two *dvarapalas*, or warriors, three lions and a three-headed elephant. They look a little the worse for wear, as well they might after the life they have led, but are actually better preserved than their contemporaries in Cambodia. These figures are reputed to have special powers that, like the Buddha figure, attract many pilgrims. It is believed that they have healing properties: touch one of the figures in a particular place and that area on your own body will receive a boost. It is said that most people rub the stomach, which is perhaps no great advertisement for

Burmese food. But the possibilities are endless: if enough of us rub the eyes then maybe an optician or two will go out of business. Plastic surgeons better watch out too, though there was no guidance on how you specified just what you wanted: a smaller nose or bigger bust. I was feeling fine so contented myself with looking from a short distance away.

I was fascinated by the gold leaf. It seemed impossible considering the gold of, say, a ring, to transform it into something so incredibly thin and flaky, and to reduce it sufficiently so that all this was financially possible too. I asked the redoubtable San about it and he simply smiled and replied, "Next Stop". We were off to visit the gold leaf workshops, and again we would find that there were a number of them located in the same street.

On the way we saw Shwe Nandaw Kyaung. This is an ornate monastery constructed entirely of teak. Originally part of the palace it survives only because it was taken to pieces and rebuilt at its current location before the palace was destroyed in World War II. Once wholly covered in gold leaf and glass mosaics it is now covered only in creosote to protect the wood, but is a substantial structure that certainly remains indicative of its former glory. Intricately carved, it must represent uncounted hours of lovingly executed work. The dark wood of its strikingly beautiful façade highlighted the bright orange of the monks' robes as they went to and fro outside and was just one of the beautiful sights of this tranquil place.

Work on so valuable a commodity as gold naturally took place in an extremely secure environment. It was like entering a prison, several doors and many locks had to be passed before we gained entry to the gold leaf workshop itself. Silent guards held large bunches of keys and small pistols. Not true. The work took place in a wooden building, much of it open-sided and we simply walked in when the bus stopped in the street outside. There were in fact several workshops, which, like other businesses we had seen elsewhere, were positioned cheek by jowl. Although fast food outlets seem to make a point of setting up next to their competitors, it seems an odd way of relating to the marketplace.

For the production of gold leaf, the starting point is about 12 grams of gold in the form of 200 pieces 2.5 by 1 centimetre in size, thin but nothing like as thin as their final form as finished gold leaf. They are placed between sheets of leather and copper plate and thinned by being pounded with a wooden mallet. After half an hour they are already larger, cut into more, smaller pieces and pounded again, this time for an hour, then, still needing to be reduced in thickness a little more, they are resized again for a final pounding. This time it is done for a full five hours. The original piece of gold makes ten in the final form and these are packed between oiled sheets of bamboo paper in packets of ten, which sell for about 400 *Kyat* (that's just one third of an American dollar so maybe our one free leaf was not so generous). Men wielding mallets like jumbo-sized baseball bats did much of the beating. It was hot, hard relentless work. The later stages apparently need to be done in a humid atmosphere and a group of woman worked in a sealed room, a kind of semi basement. We could not go in, but could watch through a window as they worked.

The noise was both loud and penetrating. San told us that some of the women went deaf after working here continuously for many years. What? I got him to repeat it to make what he said audible above the pounding. I could well believe him. A visitor had once donated some earplugs to the workers. Apparently they had tried using these to mitigate the problem, but productivity fell, as they could somehow not keep up the necessary rhythm. It was the earplugs that were abandoned. So far during my visit, the negative aspects of life in Burma had been kept firmly in the background, but this was really affecting. The job had to be done and workers liked being involved in something linked to reverence for the Buddha, but the job cannot have been very pleasant and the personal price was evidently high. Even back home I still see a mental picture of the scene through that little window if I hear any loud banging. In the modern world the prevailing economy so often dictates how people live their lives. But with this, the poor economy and need to work, combined with the religious culture, which almost universally prevailed throughout the country, to condemn these people to a task that ultimately did them no good. I had had no prior conception of the lengthy process involved in making gold leaf, much less how it affected those engaged in doing it; I wondered how many people queuing at Maha Muni Pagoda realised the human cost of the gesture they would make. If they did, then they no doubt took it for granted and gave it little thought. Gold is an inherent part of the local culture, however, and gold leaf is also put on the face to enhance beauty and even eaten to cure stomach complaints. Eating gold sounds both unpleasant and expensive, so no wonder some people prefer to rely on the healing powers of the Kymer bronze figures in Maha Muni's courtyard. As a final indication of the massive thinning that takes place to produce gold leaf, a single ounce of gold can produce gold leaf covering 12 square metres. That is, as even a size zero model would acknowledge, really, really *thin*.

Back on the road we drove past the palace in the middle of Mandalay, or rather the walls and moat. These currently do little more than front a military barracks, though there are plans to build replicas of some of the old buildings originally within the walls and a clean up and reinstatement of the moat has already been done. Renovation is a word you hear a lot here, both in terms of the treasures of the past and in more humdrum ways too. Every disaster in Burma seems to have been followed by some sort of recovery and rebuilding; comparatively recently here in Mandalay a destructive fire in 1984 led to an influx of Chinese business people who undertook rebuilding, as a preliminary to starting new businesses. You hear little about the government's role in maintaining and building the state. Imagine in Britain or America not being able to bad mouth the Prime Minister or President; people's lives just would not be the same. Any new U.K. prime minister can expect no less. Here nothing much is said and questions are ducked. I was not so bold as to ask anyone outright something like how they got on in prison, or even directly what they thought of the government. Even asking about how the nature of the government affected tourism produced only evasion. One person I spoke to just smiled, as Gi-Gi had done, and changed the subject, "I must tell you about..." This was a regular tactic. If comment is made it is done largely obliquely. More than one person told me the same story. Three of the ruling generals want to check how things stand in the country. They get a small plane to fly them across country and can see the poor villages below. One says, "I am going to drop 1,000 Kyats out of the window and make someone happy." The second, not to be outdone says, "I will drop 2,000 Kyats out and make two people happy" and the third promises to drop 10,000 and make ten people happy. At this point the pilot turns round and says, "Why don't you all just jump out and make everyone happy?" So there are feelings about the regime and the conditions stemming from it, even amongst those largely unaffected. If your life is directly at loggerheads with the regime, goodness knows how much more vehement such people feel. Meanwhile people cope, no doubt in a million ways invisible to the first time visitor. For example, as motor scooters buzzed around us, San explained why they all lacked the knee covers. "People want to resell them for the best price, when they buy them they remove the covers and when they sell them they refit them, and the machine looks like new." As I concentrated on his patient commentary I had failed to watch the traffic. Suddenly the driver's assistant, who was watching the road from his seat on the left, shouted "Go!" and the driver pulled out to overtake a slow moving pick-up truck. Only if you kept an eye on what was happening was this not unnerving.

San was on duty again in the evening back on the ship, compering when there was a fashion parade after dinner to show off the various traditional costumes of the different peoples who made up the mixed population of the country. Dinner had started with free beer and was taken looking out across the water and on to the splendid view of the lights ranged up the hill opposite. The lights twinkled as trees moved a little in the breeze in front of them. Every now and then the sound of chanting or the slow, rather melancholy tolling of bells came from the various monasteries hidden away on the dark hillside. It was an essentially peaceful sound that trickled down the hill and spilled across the water and, in a normally too noisy world, it was a pleasant one to hear in the quiet of the evening just before retiring to bed.

*

San was a hard taskmaster and had us up early in the morning. Didn't he know that this was supposed to be a holiday? On the go after an early breakfast, the air was still cool and the sun shining, so it was a good time to be out and about. We made a short walk into the village. Shwe Kyet Yet is a small village, perhaps more prosperous than some due to its proximity to the river at a point where not only *Road to Mandalay* regularly moors and has its base, but also where there is a river crossing point, ferries and a trading post. Though small it has two pagodas, both built in the 12th century, and a monastery. First we negotiated a series of narrow lanes. These were just rough earthen paths and must be treacherous in the rainy season. We moan about the rain in Britain, but then we get a goodly amount of it and some days it can rain with that British speciality, a miserable thick drizzle that seems to contain a disproportionate amount of water and can last all day; and that's just in the summer. In Burma, as in other countries in Asia affected by the monsoon, rain is a very different matter. The seasons are radically different, there may be long dry spells as coincided with this visit, but without rain the country would die. The rain may be limited to certain seasons, here mainly from May to October, and it may not rain for days on end, but when it does rain you really know about it. This rain is a primeval thing. The clouds gather, dark and ominous and then they open. They open wide. Being caught in this sort of rain is like someone upending buckets of water over your head – one after another. The water hurls itself towards the earth with a force that means that close to the ground there is as much water bouncing up as there is coming down. But after a short while, at least for routine downpours, the scene is transformed, the sun comes out, everything steams for a while and ten minutes later you would not know there had been any rain. Well, hardly know: the paths here looked like they would be muddy for a while afterwards.

Currently the lanes were bumpy but dry. Wooden houses lined either side and because of the climate their design meant that much of their structure was open. The downstairs often had few walls at all, and windows were universally open above. We could see people inside and out, washing clothes, preparing food or eating their breakfast. Other people were walking along the lanes themselves, going to work or beginning their daily rounds. We saw dogs and cats too. The cats were presumably tolerated, or indeed encouraged, to keep rats and mice at bay. I never saw a dog that appeared linked to any particular person or property, though they were not visibly malnourished; maybe the cats fed them a few scraps. The Burmese are not great pet owners.

No one seemed put out by a dozen foreigners walking though, many smiled and waved and children ran out to greet us and presented beguiling photographic opportunities for those with cameras. Photography may have been changed by the digital revolution, but so has the process of being on the receiving end and having your photo taken. Certainly the kids here were happy to pose and have their pictures taken, but they expected to be able to see the picture afterwards on the camera screen. It made a great game and their shrieks and laughter seemed to show that they were generally well pleased with the results. But then they were very photogenic and appealing, no snack monster fatties here, they spent lots of time outside and McDonalds and its ilk were nowhere to be seen. Somewhere in the material I had read about Burma was an injunction not to "spoil children with offerings of gifts or money". Among the children we saw wherever we went were some that would put out their hands hoping to be given something. The favourite gesture involved raising a hand to the mouth as if eating. It was unclear whether this was symbolic, or really meant that they wanted or needed food. Certainly no one we saw looked in any way malnourished, though there is real poverty in rural areas. What would be most appreciated was probably money or a treat like chocolate. This begging, if that is the right word, was very low-key. No one was very insistent and, with limited English ability, no lengthy case was made. I saw a few people handing over a little money to kids who had co-operated with their photography. Only once, at a temple, did we encounter anything on a more organised basis: two elderly women, their wrinkled faces the stuff of photographic prize winners, puffed on huge, loosely rolled cheroots and made it amply clear why they were there and that it was a case of "no money, no picture".

Cheroots are an inherent part of Burmese life. Smokers include men, women and children; so, no western style health education is apparently a priority here. Tobacco grows well in the country; the main centre of production is around Pakokka in the central flood plain, and cheroot manufacture is big business. The cheroots are big too, and are sometimes made up to a foot long. The tobacco used is coarse, it has herbs added to it, is boiled in palm sugar and then rolled by hand using heavy paper or maize leaves. The resultant cheroots are often smoked communally, being passed from one person to another around a group; this is a common scene in teashops. I don't know what they cost to buy, but given their rough and ready manufacture, they are presumably not too expensive as they seem to be widely favoured. Just before the trip I had started reading an excellent novel, *The Lizard Cage* by Karen Connelly, which illustrates the worst side of life in Burma and whose main protagonist is someone imprisoned in solitary confinement in a Burmese jail for writing protest songs. Solitary that is apart from ants and cockroaches, and the lizards of the title. He is allowed the occasional parcel from his family and painstakingly unwraps any cheroots included in them to find scraps of newspaper that may have been used in rolling them and on which something, however little, is still readable. He can then re-roll them to smoke. In a life utterly bereft of external stimulation, this task consumes him and any success provides a tenuous link with the distant world outside. During my time in Burma, every time I saw someone smoking a cheroot I thought of these touching scenes. Despite its gloomy topic this is an uplifting and mesmerising read, one highly recommended; after all, no journey can be truly first class without the right reading matter taken along.

On many holidays my packing consists of laying books across the bottom of the suitcase and packing anything else for which this leaves room on top. This time, in addition to *The Lizard Cage*, I had been following the latest exploits of Precious Ramotswe, she of Alexander McCall Smith's wonderful *No 1 Ladies Detective Agency* series; a delight to read and ideal for a holiday. Incidentally, I did not see Insein Prison in Yangon, but it is home to more than 10,000 prisoners, despite being built to hold a quarter of that number. It has an extremely unsavoury reputation and a regime that involves beatings for any minor infringement of the rules and a near starvation diet. If *The Lizard Cage* reflects reality, and I strongly suspect that it does, then this hardly bears thinking about.

The narrow lanes hardly gave room for traffic, but we saw several motorbikes with sidecars heaped with goods, food and more. These were mobile shops, their owners cried out as they went along in a way reminiscent of London's street criers in Charles Dickens's time and some people came out from their houses to buy their wares and have a chat – they moved the news and gossip along a bit too, I suspect. Melons were clearly in season, as every vendor seemed to have an ample supply. Just a few brick houses were slotted in amongst the simpler ones; some were really quite smart and several orders of magnitude away from the simplest of the wooden ones. "Who lives in these kinds of places?" I asked San. "Businessmen" he replied, but did not elaborate. We moved down a slight incline and could see one of the pagodas rising above the houses, its white spire shining in the early morning sun. Round the corner we could see its entrance and alongside a long line of thirty or forty monks, all with shaven heads and attired in identical looking deep red robes and with their feet bare, queued waiting to reach a large table. They all carried bowls and were collecting food. A monk only eats twice a day, once early on and again before noon. This is one of 277 rules that the monastic existence demands that you obey. They must buy nothing: only eat food given to them; communities, and certainly a village like this, readily support the system. A line of monks moving through the streets in the early morning to collect their daily rations is a common sight, and ordinary people, perhaps with little to spare, will always help to fill their bowls. Their life may be simple and Spartan, but they do not seem to go hungry.

Today, with *Road to Mandalay* at her mooring on the edge of the village, was special. The table set out had been carried here by a number of the ship's crew and was laid with bowls of food. As the monks reached the table a couple of the crew, one our jovial captain, dished out rations into their bowls. Such scenes are repeated in their essentials all across the Buddhist world. Many monks are only monks on a temporary basis. They will spend a period, maybe six months or a year or more, living as a monk, often as a kind of rite of passage as they move into adulthood. For others it is a lifetime commitment. Children may be looked after in the monastery too and in this line the last dozen or so of the queuing figures were young boys, the youngest maybe eight or nine. Even the youngest moved forward impassively just as their older brethren did. Here they will learn to read and write and also study Buddhism, meditating and chanting along with the grownups.

We watched this ritual from a discreet distance. It was a fascinating and appealing sight, one resonant with history and culture. Our presence did not appear to interfere with the proceedings, but it must surely be odd to have to get your breakfast this way, and odder still to be regularly photographed while you do it; and the ship was here every week. As the end of the line went by and the proceedings finished, I spoke to the captain, wondering if this was an onerous duty, performed only to give his passengers something to look at. But he seemed wholly genuine about it, taking it for granted just as something you do. "Small good deed. No problem. Our pleasure," he said. And a little merit gained too, if my rudimentary understanding of Buddhism is correct. We moved on, heading back out of the village by a circular route that appeared to go down the village's high street. The lane opened up on one side, the second pagoda was visible now in front of us, and beyond it we could see the river and the hills beyond on the far side of the broad stream. A few small shops formed a row alongside us interspersed with a number of the ubiquitous teashops. These were all full of people. I once read an Italian square described as looking like the result of a parking competition for the blind: it was the tangled mass of bicycles, and motorbikes and scooters outside each tea shop which brought this description to mind now.

However poor they might be in western terms, many people seemed to rate buying their breakfast at such a place very high and to be able to afford to do so every morning. Most customers were men, sitting under the roof of the open-fronted teashop of their choice and going on to work after meeting with friends in this way. There were televisions playing in them all, but this morning these were being universally ignored; even the one with a karaoke disc playing, the words of a religious song bouncing across the bottom of its screen. Cooking was being done on wood burning fires; samosas and other titbits being prepared for the no doubt regular customers who would choose which establishment to patronise by the kind of food they specialised in. The smoke and the smell of cooking drifted across the lane along with the chatter of the people.

No particular customers stood out, but I wondered if it was possible that, even in an essentially rural community like this, where everyone must know almost everyone else, some of the customers were government spies, apparently just eating their breakfast but with their ears busier than their mouths. The government's apparent need to check up on its population was legendary, so I guessed it was possible; though no one looked suspicious to me. I had heard it said that there were secret signs used by such people so that they could recognise each other. One such was said to be that these government lackeys all wore their wristwatches on their right arm. I wonder. A significant number of people are left-handed and here many people seemed not to wear a watch at all. So it seemed unlikely to be a very reliable sign, and there was no obvious indication of anything untoward. Not a single soul had "Spy" tattooed on their forehead or wore a badge saying, "Junta rules O.K." In a tiny village I would have thought anyone who sat in teashops all day and had no visible means of earning a living was probably going to be quickly spotted as one of the many people employed by the government. It was surely only those having portfolio careers: spying over breakfast, loading boats during the day and a bit more eves dropping in the evening who could hope to remain hidden.

Chapter Nine

Chapter Ten

BELL, BOOK AND CANDLE

*"Travel is the frivolous part of serious lives
and the serious part of frivolous ones."*
Anne Sophie Swethine

Our next excursion was to Mingun, a small village 10 kilometres or so further up river from our mooring place and only accessible by boat. *Road to Mandalay* was to stay put, something smaller was needed for this and the trip was billed as being by "traditional Ayerdarwady ferry". This was evidently moored a short drive away along the river straining at its mooring and eager to take us on our way. I had been wondering where people here got fuel and on the way we saw our first roadside petrol station: it consisted of a stack of large mismatched plastic containers under a rickety awning at the side of the road, but it presumably kept people moving. No wonder a good many trucks and buses seemed to carry reserve supplies. Actually, the fuel supply situation in the country is complicated. Petrol supply is rationed: people can buy only a set amount each day (two gallons when we were there) and this is not too expensive. Any more than that amount must be bought at a higher price on the black market, though this parallel economy operates wholly openly. Perhaps those "physics plants" will change everything: grow, grow!

We passed a block of sad-looking basic apartments, which San told us were part of the remuneration received by government employees. A lifetime sitting in teashops listening for any suggestions of dissent did not appear to pay too well. Actually these were not for spies, but for bureaucrats of all sorts, all of whom made only a meagre living, even counting perks such as accommodation; it was a recipe that led inevitably to widespread corruption. I had been told a tale earlier about someone in the travel business who had had to go to Singapore on business. He had sufficient money with him to cover his costs, hotel, food and so on while he was there and this cash was discovered during an ad hoc search at the airport. The official immediately demanded US$500 to let him and his money pass. He explained that unless he had the money he could not travel as, without the money, he could not afford anywhere to stay. This caused a momentary impasse, then after some haggling, they agreed on a lesser amount of US$60, which is still a considerable sum of money in Burma. He then suggested that he should put the cash in an envelope so that no one would see what the official was up to. With this agreed to, he slipped just US$10 in an envelope, sealed it up, and went hastily to get his flight, before his ruse could be discovered. "I guess it was one-all," he added. Another story involved tourists being taken to certain sights. If a fee must be paid, military personnel may be there to collect it, and they can demand a list of the tourists' passport numbers. This can take time and everyone must have his or her passport number to hand. One guide told me, "I always use the same list of totally fictitious names and numbers. I have no idea what happens to the records, but they never seem to be checked." Somewhere in government circles, there must be an official who believes that practically every westerner who visits

Burma is called Smith. Probably such incidents are an everyday occurrence and, given the situation that prevails, such small victories doubtless provide disproportionate pleasure, and are something to recount in the tea shops. This was all told to me in a you-can-beat-the-system kind of way; but sometimes, one fears, such incidents must end in tears.

Pulling up alongside another area of moored boats, we soon found that "traditional ferry" meant a double decker boat about 50 foot in length. It had an open top deck and the look of something that had been sailed on the river for centuries by a skipper without the words maintenance or renovation in his vocabulary. We had to traverse a gangway and then cross two other similar boats to reach it. At the gangway we were urged to "Please hold onto rail", though the rail was just a loose bamboo pole held alongside the gangway by two men, one at each end. Nevertheless we all boarded safely. I checked out the lower deck, where a huge engine sat totally unscreened, its various moving parts a potential hazard that would have had Health and Safety officers at home apoplectic with indignation and forbidding our even going on board never mind any sort of voyage. Here too was the toilet, the kind of thing that makes my wife say, "I think I'll wait." Men really do have an easier life than women in some respects (or is it most?). Minguin was an hour away and, sitting up on the top deck in chairs a few decades younger than the boat, it was an hour that passed by very pleasantly.

The breeze as we went along mitigated the heat somewhat and the view along the river was, as ever, fascinating. I saw two small boats being pulled along by women walking on the river path, a man sitting in the stern steering to find them a good, safe course. Another sign of how far removed we were from any sign of women's lib; though maybe the men did the pulling on the return trip, which would be against the current, to make up for having it easy this time. I did not mention this to my wife, who I know would have replied in "fat chance" mode. Keen to explore everything I went to speak to the man at the helm; captain seems too grand a word to use, though apart from his wife and his young son, who was maybe six years old, he was in sole charge. The wheelhouse was empty of anything other than a wheel with a chain running round it. This disappeared on down through a ragged hole in the floor to the lower deck. Turn the wheel and the chain moved and linked up in some convoluted way below that moved the rudder. There were no instruments or other controls of any sort. Having steered the *Road to Mandalay* for a few minutes, something of this simplicity should surely be a doddle; so I asked if I could have a go. The helmsman, who apparently spoke minimal English, just nodded, then turned and walked to the back of the wheelhouse and began speaking to his wife. Supervision was evidently not in his vocabulary either. I kept to the same course, only turning a little as another slightly smaller boat heading the other way came so close it looked like they were going to board us. I glared at these pirates as we passed, but no cutlasses were evident and they just smiled and waved as we passed each other. I must have looked an unlikely looking skipper to them; but maybe that is what caused the smiles. Unlike *Road to Mandalay* this boat was instantly responsive; a tiny turn on the wheel was translated into instant movement on the water. It would have been fun to zoom to and fro a bit, but the helmsman arrived back at my elbow and my turn ended.

Up on the top deck it was time to shop again. A table was laid out by the helmsman's wife and on it were spread a variety of goods: the ubiquitous *longyi*, other clothes and jewellery. It was rather like the duty free goods trolley coming round on an aeroplane. Many of the women descended like locusts despite the fact that we had seen similar things at every stop, and the most dedicated shopaholics went away with more packages. What were some of these women going to do with everything, I wondered. One *longyi* as a souvenir I could understand; perhaps some of them planned to open a shop. Perhaps they are saleable on e-Bay, though I hope not as I might have missed out on a fortune. Maybe, if I ever see *Longyis-R-Us* open in the States, I will be able to say I witnessed its birth. Soon we could see Minguin in the distance ahead of us. Buildings were visible straggling along the shore and up a small hill behind, with the inevitable pagoda shapes behind. Gradually we got nearer and on arrival there were no jetties or moorings visible, but our helmsman simply rammed the boat into the sandy shore, ran out the gangway, its bamboo rail manned and held steady by people ashore who came to help. This proved to be a place well attuned to its tourist visitors, though more of these were locals on a day out than foreigners like us. There were stalls on the beach, and a number of carts with two side seats under canvas awnings and two oxen harnessed to them bearing signs saying "Taxi", lined up waiting to take those unable to walk a few hundred yards up to the village. The first part of the street we walked along was lined with tea shops and various other shops, most of which sold pictures, predominantly oil paintings, but also some watercolours. It was no surprise that temples, pagodas and monks featured a good deal in these but, though the colours were bold, the quality was somewhat crude and I saw nothing I would have wanted to live with. This was sad, as I think a picture makes a satisfying souvenir. Speedy production and low price seemed to overcome any real desire to excel, something which was in contrast with the high quality of workmanship seen in other craft and artistic areas such as the lacquer ware.

The village was strung primarily along the one street, which ran for most of a mile. The main points of interest here were the world's largest working bell and Bodawpaya's pagoda. That's not counting the many simple shops, which again our more shopaholic fellow travellers seemed to find irresistible. There were those who came back from every trip laden with packages. They must have suitcases the size of a small house, though with Air Mandalay's smaller than usual luggage allowance, I wondered how they would fly it all out. Remembering our landing I did actually hope they stuck to the limit, as landing more heavily laden than we had been on the way in might push the limits.

San wanted us to see the bell. How interesting can a bell be, I wondered? Well, actually very: this one is 3.7 metres high, that's as high as two men one standing on top of the other, 5 metres across at its mouth and it weighs a mammoth 87 tons. That's not just a lot, it's a weight equivalent to 25 decent sized elephants and even one of those can do some damage if it stands on your toes! This is a very serious bell indeed, and more than enough to put all thoughts of bragging out of other bells' minds. It dates from 1790 and stands back from the dusty road near to a large convalescent home for homeless people, mainly the elderly left without relatives. King Bodawpaya had it cast to grace the huge

Mingun Pagoda, a structure that he intended to be the largest pagoda on earth. To cast something so huge in those days was a feat of unique craftsmanship and the king, realising this, rewarded the maker by having him executed so that the feat could never be repeated. Hard times for architects and bell casters, and who knows how much larger a bell the poor guy might have been able to make if he had not been cut off in his prime.

In 1838, a year when a major earthquake did damage throughout Burma, the bell was dislodged as its wooden supports collapsed with shock. Today, pristine and undamaged by the fall, it is hung from strong iron rods and is the largest working bell in the world. There is in fact a larger one in Russia's Kremlin, but that cracked on casting and has never sounded a clear note, though the Russians still rate it highly. Here beneath its wooden shelter the Mingun bell not only hangs proudly, its rim about three feet of the ground, but also works well. Heavy wooden batons lay on the ground nearby, and a crowd of smiling, bright-eyed children hung around it only to pleased to explain to visitors just where you hit it to get the best sound. This is a couple of hands' breadths up from the rim, in case you are wondering.

One more thing, if you are brave enough to duck underneath you will find the entire inside surface covered with graffiti. The writing is mainly Burmese, of course, but some has been left by visitors, and much of it, like graffiti everywhere, is no doubt either obscene, intended to be humorous in a lavatorial sort of way or simply the equivalent of *Kilroy was here*. Naturally I do not approve of graffiti in most contexts, though I love what the writer Alan Bennett said about it, "Mark my words, when a society has to resort to the lavatory for its humour, the writing is on the wall." I wondered what topics appealed to Burmese graffiti writers. Perhaps there was one here based on the old one saluting the police: *God made animals great and small, some that slither, some that crawl – and Burma's police employ them all.* Did the largely Buddhist population favour another old favourite, *Reincarnation is making a comeback?* Maybe there were some I would like. My favourite is *Insanity is hereditary, you get it from your children*; I like it because it makes me smile and besides, I can vouch for its accuracy. Perhaps some lacked confidence like that expressed by another classic: *My inferiority complexes aren't as good as yours.* I crawled briefly to look underneath, terrified as I did so that at that precise moment the bell would decide to drop and chop off my leg. Or worse, so that I went out with a ringing in more than just my ears. The quantity of material written inside was huge, but nothing new registered at a glance from the few in English and I quickly effected a judicious retreat.

What sort of structure was this behemoth destined for? We walked on and went to see the Minguin or Mantara Gyi Pagoda. This was certainly the most ruined structure we visited, but it was also undoubtedly amongst the most impressive. It was no surprise that a King was involved: at the time its building began King Bodawpaya was at the peak of his powers and wanted the world to know it. His vision for the giant pagoda came following a visit from a Chinese delegation in 1790, which gave him a tooth of the Buddha as a gift; the man must have had the most extraordinary number of body parts as such relics seem to crop up just about everywhere around the Buddhist world. Naturally the King was delighted with this and obviously had to have somewhere to put it, so rather than just hide it under his pillow and wait for the tooth fairy, he moved his home to Ayeyarwady and spent the next seven years supervising the building of a suitable home for the tooth. His design specified a structure 150 feet high, and an army of thousands of slave labourers was recruited to work on the building. As work progressed rumours somehow started saying that if ever the huge structure were to be finished the country would be ruined. Despite this and various other distractions like building the enormous Meiktila Dam and fighting the first Anglo-Burmese war, he kept doggedly on. The tooth alone was not enough to be the centrepiece of his dream. It is said that the shrine room where the tooth was put also contained 40,000 other objects, many of them gold and silver. This was not a man to do things by halves. He also put in a machine for making soda water, just invented and imported from England, so if that appealed to him goodness knows what other things he chose. Choose he did though, and then the room was sealed.

Thereafter the economy shrank and with it his wealth and construction was thus abandoned. He died in 1813, and his successors and family never restarted the project. Despite having 122 children and over 200 grandchildren there must have been something hideously off putting about it, as not one of them saw fit to lay even one single additional brick. So, the pagoda was thus left unfinished, at just one third of its intended height. Nearby a small replica, the Pondawpaya, provides a further insight into how it might have been. The unfinished building was then damaged in the 1838 earthquake so that it partly collapsed; long cracks are still visible, even so it remains an inspiring sight. The intended size is clear, and the shape of two huge lions that were to be on guard alongside and to the front of the pagoda remain apparent. Each lion was constructed from more than 800,000 bricks. It is not difficult to imagine how it all might have been. Given the time he must have spent siring children, what a vision King Bodawpaya had, and what a pity circumstances conspired to prevent its realisation. Despite the time that has passed, luckily what remains provides us with tantalising hints of his intentions.

Set high above the river the pagoda surveys the surrounding countryside and is said to give the best view for miles around; so naturally San suggested we climb to the top. A good number of the group declined, mopped their brows and went to find somewhere shady to sit down, but a few took up the challenge. Given my intention to write about it, naturally I had to go up. I lost count of the steps after the first hundred, at which point I doubt I was even half way up, and I lost my breath and most of my will to live too as I went on. After the first few, the steps were uneven, all of different heights, and very steep. Weeds grew from the many cracks around the path, and some substantial plants had taken root in the larger fissures resulting from the earthquake damage. But the view from the top was staggering. It was a clear, bright and sunny day and I could see for miles. The wide river stretched across the view from side to side, the *Road to Mandalay* appearing as a tiny, but recognisable, dot on the far bank a little to the right. Pagodas were strewn like jewels across the hillside and across the surrounding countryside away into the distance.

Amongst the buildings that are laid out in front of you as you perch atop what has been called the biggest pile of bricks in the world is the shining white Hsinbyume or Myatheindan Pagoda. This is based on Buddhist cosmology with seven concentric terraces guarded by five kinds of mythical monster, though possibly their effectiveness as guards has been reduced as most of them have had their heads stolen, which must make their spotting any unsavoury characters a touch difficult. However, it is the scale of what is around that impresses, a profusion of temples and towers ranged across the landscape, a testament to the massive egos of their builders, all trying to outdo their predecessors and clock up a powerful amount of merit to see them reincarnated successfully. It seems an odd system, but given the beliefs, one can see the attraction. It would be galling to say the least to wake up reincarnated as a lowly cockroach knowing that all that would have been necessary to move you further up the cosmic scale of things was some additional dollops of cement and just a little more bricklaying.

If going up the steps was hard work, coming down felt downright dangerous, a sensation compounded by my variable focus glasses, which meant I had to squint down at a contrived angle to see each next oddly spaced step clearly. I arrived at the foot of the stairway feeling hot and with pains in my calves, but it was a worthwhile climb and the view is something that will remain with me for a long time.

We walked back to the ferry through the length of the village. It was hot now and we were not the only ones feeling it. We watched a child buying an iced lolly. Flakes of ice were shaved off a large block with a knife more suited to conquest than confectionery. A dollop of red fruit jelly was added to the mass of flaked ice and all this was then wrapped in coconut leaves and squeezed tight in the maker's hands to mould it into a coherent lump, rather as someone might squeeze a snowball before throwing it. A stick was added and, hey presto, an iced lolly was the result. The child beamed, handed over a coin or two and went off down the path well pleased. Some simple pleasures are universal.

Back on the beach we boarded the ferry, using the same sort of handheld rail alongside the gangway to guide us aboard. Knowing we would return hot, iced drinks and cold towels were immediately on hand to cool us down as soon as we settled back on the top deck. In such a climate, even walking a couple of miles seems tiring for someone unused to the heat and it was a pleasant respite to sit comfortably on the ferry as it made its way back along the river and across to the other shore. It was quiet, with most of the sound of our engine disappearing astern, and people chatted or, in one or two cases, dozed. Just occasionally another, usually smaller, boat passed the other way, a raucous motor necessitating a pause in conversation while it went on its way. Again simple sights along the way were fascinating: a small boat with its solitary fisherman manhandling a net laid in a circle and kept afloat by a row of plastic bottles; a herd of cattle being led to the river's edge to drink; washing laid out to dry flat on the ground. Some small boats had sails; indeed with the wind normally blowing up river sails provide useful assistance in going against the current. The feeling of openness and being away from everything was pronounced, the river was broad, its shining surface disappeared into a blue-grey misty background at the edge of our vision. The sky was huge. It was a sky to put things in perspective, the sort of sky to look up at and forget your worries. In the United States the state of Montana is known as the Big Sky State: perhaps Burma deserves to be known as the Big Sky Country. The time sped by and soon we could see our destination and signs of the town ahead; a large, currently immobile, Ferris wheel towered above a play area for children, and was easily the tallest structure in view.

Back where we had started, our boat pulled in alongside two others and we climbed ashore and walked through the crowds busy getting goods and people to and from the boats on the wide beach. Our bus driver and his left-hand-side-lookout were waiting for us and we were soon on our way again. Our bus may not have been the newest in the world, but it ran well and never let us down. Not so every vehicle. Throughout the trip we regularly saw vehicles of every sort stalled at the roadside. Sometimes it was a puncture, the rough roads and worn tyres taking their toll. Often a raised bonnet showed it was something mechanical and there appeared to be a thriving trade in patch-you-up-mechanics. We regularly passed small huts at the roadside, maybe the size of two telephone boxes, doors open at the front, their inside walls hung neatly with every sort of tool imaginable. If, or perhaps it should be when, someone did break down then assistance was never far away for the driver who needed some help. It seemed likely that drivers here, certainly those for whom driving was a necessary part of earning their living, knew a good deal more practical mechanics than is now usually the case in the west. Certainly in England, nothing ever seems to go wrong with a car that can actually be *repaired*. Whenever I have a puncture, albeit a rare occurrence these days, some teeth sucking is always followed by my being told it is, "No, no... not safe to repair that, you'll need a new tyre on there, governor." An ailing engine is coupled up to some sort of computer diagnostic system and its owner is then told what proportion of it needs replacing. When the alarm and locking system on my car failed recently it was not mended, it was reprogrammed. Nothing is made to work by being given a good kick, and precious little is done without a cost that is considerably more than I paid for my first car. My first car was an early Mini. A great little car, and oh the joy of being independently mobile for the first time, but when it rained the distributor seized up and you had to lie on the road, reach under the car and dry it off. At the time no one thought this strange. In the time warp that is Burma this kind of situation remains, and indeed is considered, normal, but perhaps the fact that the cars are all old, and don't have fuel injection systems and computer controlled this and that, makes them easier to repair and keep on the road. Go on working they certainly seem to.

Chapter Eleven

OVER THE BRIDGE

"... a bridge over troubled water."

Paul Simon

Some of our expeditions had us driving across the Inwa Bridge; despite our indulgences we did not evidently add up to a weight that consigned our bus to the ferry. At each end of the bridge there was a military post, but when our bus was stopped, nothing more sinister was involved than paying a crossing fee. The military juggernaut was apparently so huge that it had men to spare to run a simple toll bridge; maybe there was a special rank, Private First Class Road Barrier Opener-and-Shutter, because for one man this seemed the extent of his task. I bet it makes him proud: "What did you do today, soldier?" his friends must ask and he replies, "Today I collected from 210 cars, 16 buses and a motor-cycle with a sidecar full of piglets – I charged extra for each and every piglet too." Maybe he did have more sinister, though less obvious purpose too. Or perhaps we should just be grateful that he was kept too busy to have time for any less pleasant tasks. We were not held up. The bus slowed to a stop, the driver's assistant leapt out, ran to the kiosk where the toll was paid and returned after a moment with a small ticket. The driver started forward when he saw him returning and he jumped onto the moving bus.

As we drove on we passed a tree. "So what?" you might say. This one, a banyan tree towering fifty-feet tall and spreading its branches to shade the traffic, grew in the middle of the road. The road bulged out around it in a tight little circle to left and right so that traffic could pass either side. This seems odd but was easily explained. The tree was home to a *nat* and local people would not allow the tree to be felled in case the *nat* was displeased, as well it might be, I suppose, if its home of many years was cut from under it. We saw several like it on our travels and it was yet another sign of the unique nature of the local culture. Maybe it is an idea to adopt at home. I rather like the idea of the public enquiry considering a bypass foundering on the impossibility of disturbing a local *nat*. In these days of political correctness and respect for the beliefs of others, maybe it could happen.

While there was running water in the towns, for many people in villages and smaller communities along the Ayeradwady, the river is their only source of water. They will bathe in it and take their clothes to wash at its margin, but they also need water at home. A special kind of pot is almost universally used for this and we went to see them being made. In a village on the far side of the river we visited a pottery. The pots were made in traditional fashion on a wheel, this one set at ground level. A lump of clay was whacked down and as the wheel spun, the potters used their hands to mould it into the right shape. I don't know why it surprised me, but the wheel was hand powered. Thus two women, the patient women again, squatted on the ground: one of them kept the wheel turning, while the other worked the pot. Finishing them involved beating them to make them larger, a job done while holding something inside the pot to mould it to the right shape. Firing them also had no need of anything high tech. A huge pile of straw was laid on the ground. Within this up to a thousand pots were placed and more straw piled on the top. This was sufficiently damp that it burnt for a long time creating a fierce heat inside and finishing off the pots to the required standard. At one point, one of the women had to move some finished pots away from the work area. She squatted down and, after putting a wound-up length of material on her head to create a flat surface, she piled five pots on top of her head and disappeared off down a lane. In use, these pots are filled from the river, a river that runs clean but is heavy with silt, and so the water is then left for several days to allow the sediment to settle. A chain of several pots is used, with each at a different stage of settling: one just filled and others down the line actually being used for drinking water.

All this pot-making took place in an earthen-floored courtyard amongst the village houses, and was repeated in many other places in this village and others. The pots were then brought together to a central point only for firing and then sent off for sale and distribution. It was truly a cottage industry. Because it was being done just in a village square, the area became a kind of social centre. People came and went; or came, stopped and chatted and went. One potter handed over to another as their shifts changed, and the children played amidst all the activity. The kids were apparently delighted to see us, after all when you have seen one pot made, you have seen them all and any distraction to routine was no doubt welcome. The older children looked after the younger ones and despite the basic life they must lead they were all smiling and laughing. As with other groups of children, being photographed was again a big thing. They pushed to the front of the group to get in shot. They posed shamelessly and always wanted to see the result on the little digital screen that most cameras sported. If you travel to Burma and still favour an old fashioned roll of film, prepare to be one seriously unpopular tourist, at least with the youngest generation of the people you meet.

Another craft for which the Burmese are renowned is the manufacture of silverware. Manufacture is perhaps the wrong word, it is a traditional craft and again is organised as a cottage industry with production spread primarily around many small workshops and involving hundreds of families. Burmese silverware has been famous since the thirteenth century, and bowls, vases, boxes and items of jewellery are still made in the traditional way. Daggers and their sheaths used to be a regularly made item too. Most items are embossed and engraved and the quality of this embellishment is superb.

Burmese names are a trifle odd. They can consist of two or three words and do not distinguish man or woman, married or single or even indicate if people belong to the same family. Rather oddly, they can also be changed on a whim. Well, not so much on a whim, usually after a long and complicated consultation with monks, soothsayers or astrologers, something that also happens when a child is first named. One factor, hence the astrologer, is that a person's day of birth is important here and can often be detected because it is made apparent by their name. I did ask how this worked, but the long explanation was so multi-layered and complex that I gave up and will make no attempt to describe it here, other than to say that one of the complications is that there are actually eight days in the week in Burma. That is to say, in this context there are two Wednesdays. Which "bit" of

Wednesday you are born on makes a difference too: Wednesday birth is linked to the elephant, which either have tusks and are volatile, or are without tusks and thus calm. Confused? I was and still am. The link between all this and silverware is that many of the designs and symbols used in the traditional engraving are linked to the days of the week on which people are born. Thus, with a christening looming in the family, and silver being traditional, if a little old fashioned, for christening presents in Britain, we bought something inscribed with elephants. So, if you grow up and read this Fabian (your first mention in print), it was selected because you were born on a Wednesday. Elephants are lucky too, which I guess makes their day a good one to be born on. In Thailand the image of an elephant is regarded as lucky only if it has its trunk raised, in Burma it is regarded as lucky however it is holding its trunk, a fact that must increase their influence for good luck quite a bit.

Seeing the craftsmanship in action was a wonder to behold. How do you get the image of an elephant, or indeed anything else for that matter, onto a piece of metal? Well, its simple - you clout it with a hammer. Okay, there is wax used, differences between how something is hit from one side or the other depending on whether the effect is to be concave or convex, but whatever it is destined to look like you hit it using a hammer and tiny chisel. There's hitting and hitting, of course. So you cannot just bash at it every which way, of course; the trick is to hit it just right - and being able to do that no doubt takes many years of training and practice. The accuracy and precision of the craftsmen and women we saw in action that day was astounding. Those experienced and proficient in the trade can make an elephant appear in what seems like seconds, though the final piece then needs a lot of polishing to create the final finish and effect. And that, needless to say, means still more patient women.

It was time to move on and meet some rather different patient women.

*

The nun was eighty-six years old and spoke not a word of English. Barely five foot in her flat sandals, she was dressed in a simple pink and orange robe, her head shaved, her face a deep brown and wrinkled like a walnut and she was wearing gold-rimmed spectacles which appeared to be a size too big for her face. She was the leader of a community of more than 100 nuns, had lived in the cluster of wooden buildings we were visiting since she was nine years old, and her vitality was as obvious as the nose on her face. There was no doubting her welcome. She smiled. She beamed; and she smiled some more. Her smile lit up the shady courtyard. She gestured that we should look around.

Our bus had stopped and we had walked away from the road up a rough earthen lane lined with buildings to see where these nuns lived. They and their home, the Zeyar Theingi Nunnery, were supported by donations, one rich benefactor having long ago given them the buildings they occupied, and here they lived a simple, devotional life. We took off our shoes and went up a flight of wooden steps outside the largest building. The whole of the top floor was one open area and the younger nuns used it as classroom. It was cool inside. The many windows surrounding it were all open to the air. About twenty young nuns were currently there, sitting on the polished wooden floor spread around the large room arranged in groups of four or five, all engaged in a soft ritual chanting to learn verbatim the religious texts that they were studying. It seemed to work too. Very few were following the pages in front of them and many seemed to have already successfully committed the words to memory. Good old-fashioned learning by rote. Maybe in England more children would be able to multiply in their heads if they still learnt their multiplication tables in the same way rather than reaching for a calculator. How often do you go into a shop these days and it takes five minutes for the young person serving to find a calculator, work out the simplest sum and give you your change? In large stores it is all computerised, of course, but that is no excuse, they should... sorry, it's a bit of a hobbyhorse, some kids would learn more in a school of fish. But apologies, I digress.

It was difficult to tell the girls apart as all were of a similar age, had shaved heads and were dressed in the standard issue robes; certainly they wore no makeup or had any individual adornment to differentiate them one from another. They acknowledged our visit with smiles, but paused not at all in their task. When we went back down the stairs I noticed that about 20 pairs of seemingly identical black flip-flops were ranged around the bottom of the steps. How did they find their own pair, I wondered? Maybe in such a sharing community it did not matter. It was afternoon and at 4:30 p.m. precisely a gong sounded and a number of the novices came down to prepare food. Most of their rice and basic supplies were collected as donations – a collection being made every two days - and there was a cooking rota so that they took turns. We were able to look at the kitchen, a room with no windows, but an open door and its walls hung with utensils and with the paraphernalia for producing simple meals ranged around. Routine seemed to be the order of the day. We had seen timetables posted in the upstairs classroom and hardly a minute of the day, from the time they got up very early in the morning until they went to bed, was not accounted for in some way. They were not totally isolated, of course, people came and went and they interacted with the community, but even so however worthy it is, it must be a very insular way of life. For anyone unconvinced by religion, it is surely very difficult to understand. Given the respect given to all things religious here, however, though it was undoubtedly hard work, it was also a reasonably safe and comfortable way of life. One might observe that in many ways those there did not know what they were missing, though also that in the West teenage girls would be obsessed with such essentials as makeup, clothes, reality television and teenage boys. The predominant feeling given, however, was that they were happy with their lot. If you can measure happiness with smiles, then they were very happy.

We left them smiling and waving goodbye and the bus took us to our next stop. This was the Kuthodaw Pagoda. We might be beginning to suffer from a surfeit of pagoda visiting, but this one, set at the bottom of Mandalay Hill, is truly remarkable. Inside its substantial outer wall is a central structure, Maha Lawka Marazein Pagoda, which is 30 metres high and was built in 1857 as a smaller representation of the famous Shwezigon Pagoda near Bagan. This is an impressive entity in its own right, but has no less than 729 individual small pagodas, added to the place in 1872 during the Fifth Buddhist Synod, surrounding it. These are constructed in white marble, are all about ten foot high and are ranged in orderly rows. Each one has a small chamber within it that contains a large inscribed marble tablet. Why? Here is housed what is known as the world's largest book.

The teachings of Buddha are recorded in various canons, or collections of scripture. Initially they existed only through an oral tradition; chanting was originally just a way of ensuring this tradition was kept fresh and passed on. This *Tipitaka* was first written down in Sri Lanka, as long ago as the first century BC. It consists of three parts (or *pitaka)*. First, there are the sermons of the Buddha or *sutta picada,* secondly the rules of monastic discipline or *vinaya pitaka,* and thirdly the scholastic treatises or *abhidhamma pitaka,* which were added later. It all adds up to a whole lot of words. And each and every one of those words has been carved onto marble tablets and it is these that were then housed in the small pagodas. When this was done it was the first time the texts had been recorded in the Pali script, Pali being a vernacular language related to Sanskrit. At this point I am only part way through writing this book and what remains seems to me to require a significant number of further words. In one sense it is a daunting prospect. You may be worse and resent having to write even a short note. But this was a truly monumental task. It was one that took many months of work and employed more than two and a half thousand monks, all devoted Buddhist scholars as well as skilled stonemasons, to complete the job. What a noise it must have made as that many hammers rose and fell. It must have sounded like a vast horde of demented woodpeckers on acid. I get upset if my next-door neighbour mows the grass on a quiet afternoon. This must have driven the neighbours mad on an industrial scale, and been made worse by the time it took. It is bad enough complaining about a loud party next door and being told that everyone will be gone in a couple of hours. It must have been worse here, "Noise? Oh don't worry about it, we'll be done by the end of next year." I wonder though if it was the done thing to express outrage at being disturbed by the undertaking of so worthy a task. When first carved, the letters were all veneered in gold leaf, though this has gone over the ages and not been replaced.

San was, as always, eager to get the full import of everything across to us. He told us not only that if you set out to read every tablet, then doing so reading at a normal reading pace throughout every day of the week it would still take you a full year and three more months to read the text right through. That certainly puts popping out to the library for half an hour in a whole new perspective. It also gives readers a perfect excuse to put things off: "Sure I'll repaint the kitchen for you, dear. Just let me finish reading this first." Now all this may go back to the late 1800s, but it is a task that some people still undertake today. Given the time it takes, I am not sure why anyone would do that. Maybe it's a kind of penance, and if so the Buddhists have a punishment system that makes others look a little tame. Consider the Roman Catholics. You can hardly compare having to recite a mere couple of Hail Marys after confessional with more than a year of solitary reading. Again, as with so many things in Burma, the commitment to things religious is awesome. People are not just respectful of it. In the past, and to a degree today too, some people have literally dedicated their entire lives to it and done so in their many thousands. Few other religions have left such extensive physical evidence of ancient works in this way.

From the largest book in the world we went to one of the highest hill tops around, and our bus took the long switchback road up to the summit of Sagaing. It did so with a certain hesitation, juddering a little on the many steep corners, but it did it, sending a few pedestrians and cyclists hurrying to the edge of the narrow road as it went. I was glad we met nothing our size coming down. At the top we stopped alongside the Sun U Ponya Shin Pagoda. Yes, another one, but in this case it was to be the last of our visit. This whole area consists of a series of hills, the highest topped with the pagoda just mentioned. Many Burmese consider Sagaing to be the centre of the Buddhist faith for the whole country, and across its hills are spread more than 600 monasteries, home to some 5,000 monks. In addition, there are countless temples and pagodas. The hills are a picture: with shining towers of gold and white standing proud of a hillside green with trees and with splashes of colour added by frangipani and other flowering plants. Houses and other smaller buildings show less readily through the vegetation. The quietness of the area is broken only by occasional traffic noises if you are near the road and something is struggling up the hill; and by the intermittent sound of bells, chanting and cymbals occasionally audible from the monasteries. Because the place is a destination for pilgrims as well as local people visiting one or other of the shrines, many people come here and many of them walk, patiently climbing the hill and doing so slowly to mitigate the heat of the day. Every so often on the ascent earthen pots are set out in the shade of trees to assist thirsty travellers make it to the top without the need of an intravenous drip on arrival. Some of the main pagodas, which are set away from the road, have long, sometimes zigzagging walkways snaking across the hillside to give access to them and these are covered to protect their visitors from the sun. Given that many local people will have a favourite shrine that they will visit every day, you would have to be fit to choose one located far up the hill.

This pagoda is like many others, consisting of a central stupa, a series of terraces and having the mandatory large Buddha figure sitting inside. The place sticks in the mind primarily because of the tiling of its terrace floors. Obviously not original, the tiles were an eclectic mix of near fluorescent colours, mainly pale pink and lime green. They would have made the bathroom from hell. Maybe it seemed like a good idea at the time, maybe there was a dire need for refurbishment, maybe they were a job lot and some minor official was measured more on his management of the budget than the aesthetics of his decisions. Maybe they had the mother of all colour blindness. Who knows? Why ever they may have been laid, the effect was spectacularly horrid. Inside there was the usual array of statues: candles burnt, incense filled the air and local visitors paid homage in their favourite spots around the complex. Around the walls, as in so many such places, there were framed photographs of high ranking junta figures paying homage to the Buddha. Any number of portraits portraying Attila the Hun knitting would not have rewritten history's assessment of him, and I fancy that those depicted here delude themselves if they think that a single member of the population likes the government anymore because they seek to portray themselves thus.

But this is not regarded as an exceptional pagoda; it is just located in an exceptional spot. Like the view from Minguin pagoda further to the North, the vista here was a sight to behold. The entire countryside was laid out before us, the river running through it from right to left as you looked. In the late afternoon the river was like a silver thread across one's vision, and from several hundred feet above it what appeared to be tiny boats moved about their business on its surface. Already the mistiness that is usual in the evenings was making the sky slightly hazy and it gave the whole scene a characteristic tone. We sat for a while just soaking up the view, though a mere glance at something like this would be sufficient to lodge it securely in the memory. But we could not linger to watch the approaching sunset.

San had somewhere else in mind for us to do that on what was to be our last evening here in Mandalay.

Chapter Eleven

Chapter Twelve

A LITTLE MORE TO DO

*"Countries, like people, are
loved for their failing."*

F Yeats Brown

In 1782 King Bodawpaya built the city of Amarpura, or
rather he moved the city of Ava on the advice of Manipurian
astrologers. When Bodawpaya came to the throne it was after
a power struggle, a massacre and the destruction of a sizeable
village, Paungga, where the king had the entire population
burned. It sounds a less than happy time and he appears to
have made a somewhat stormy accession; the astrologers
worried about it, as well they might, and were at pains to
suggest something that would mitigate further disaster. They
must have felt they had to make a dramatic gesture and
moving a city was the obvious answer. So that is what they
recommended and in May 1783 all the inhabitants of Ava
packed their bags and moved to Amarapura. There were
some 200,000 people involved in the move so they probably
didn't all move on the same day, that would have taxed even
the largest removal company, but in due course everyone was
set up in their new homes and presumably life went on. The
king's palace was at the centre, of course. He had had a
modest pad built: the wall round it ran for more than a
kilometre and a half and there was a striking pagoda at each
corner to keep it safe.

You would think that, after all this, he would rest easy for a while. But, no, in due course the city was partly torn down with many of the wooden buildings being re-sited in Mandalay, the river was diverted to flood the city and it was only much later in 1841 that a subsequent king, King Tharrawaddy, resettled it and then ... Enough, surely no other country has such a history: changing names, moving cities, rerouting rivers, changing rulers and with fights, massacres and invasions interspersed throughout. Today Amarpura is home to a few tens of thousands of people, and is a centre for the weaving of cotton and silk. It is here where most of the country's festival clothing is made; another cottage industry with the work spread around many homes, families and small workshops, a loom in every room. Bronze work is a speciality too and many of the country's statues were cast here. The old royal palace is long gone; though the pagodas once sited at its corners all remain and give evidence of its extent. Here too is one of the largest monasteries in Burma. Well over a thousand monks live here, their numbers often swelled by pilgrims and visitors during festivals. Like other monks they eat only what is donated to them and as collection is done as a group activity the line so formed here must be a sight to behold. Sometimes a single donor contributes the food for a day. With so many monks the cost of such is significant, but the merit gained by the donor from so doing is huge, and it is said that there is a waiting list of donors waiting their turn. This may seem to western eyes to be a strange system, but to see it occurring, as we did when *Road to Mandalay's* crew organised a collection point in the village at which the ship moors, is curiously moving. A final oddity is that any generosity received is never acknowledged in any way. It is the tradition that the food is taken without visible acknowledgement or a word of thanks being spoken.

All that said, the area is most famous for Lake Taungthaman, a large stretch of water which lies just to the South, and for the unique wooden U Bein Bridge, which stretches across it for over a kilometre, and was built using teak wood taken from Amarapura when it was abandoned over two hundred years ago. It is wide enough only for people, bicycles and the occasional hand pushed cart. It takes a quarter of an hour or more to walk across the bridge and there are regular covered staging posts to provide a shady place to catch your breath on the way. The Lake is shallow and much of it virtually disappears in the dry season leaving productive soil that is soon, if temporarily, cultivated. Fishermen here forego boats for much of the year and simply wade into the water, sometimes only waist high or less, to lay their nets. The bridge has a very evocative silhouette and many people know its profile because it was featured on the cover of a bestselling book, *The Glass Palace* by Amitav Ghosh, a novel which starts at the time of the British invasion of 1885 and the taking of Mandalay and spans a hundred years and many Asian countries.

Because of its fame, this is certainly a tourist sight as well as a much-used thoroughfare. When we pulled up, parking on what in the wet season would be the bottom of the lake, and the bus disgorged its passengers we found stalls selling souvenirs and were quickly surrounded by hawkers young and old selling clothes, jewellery and ornaments. They were the most pushy we had encountered so far and needed some discouraging, though the most shopaholic of our fellow travellers needed no second invitation and were quickly into a little haggling. Negotiation of this sort is best conducted in a way that gives it some time, but a few minutes later they were retreating laden with packages wrapped in old newspapers.

At the end of the bridge where we were, set a couple of hundred metres back from the lake, was – guess what – a pagoda. The sunset behind it, its profile and the evening colours in the sky created a scene to make any photographer drool. I walked a few hundred metres out along the rickety bridge. I had to avoid holes in the woodwork and move gingerly around planks that seemed on the verge of dropping off, and tread carefully too as there are no side rails and the walkway was 12 – 15 metres from the ground or the water when I ventured further out. A constant procession of people went to and fro, many carrying bags and bundles of various sorts. This was the end of the day and it was clear that most people were hurrying home from whatever work or errand had taken them to the other side of the lake. At the end as I returned and stepped off the bridge I saw amongst the stalls of various sorts that several people were selling live birds. Some were small and were I presume bought by people who released them to engender good luck as I have seen happening with birds, and fish too, in Thailand and elsewhere. Amongst them were some larger birds, including some beautiful owls. These were very like the English Barn Owl or the one that acts as postman and delivers Harry Potter's mail (which is actually a snowy owl). I hated to see them imprisoned in a tiny cage, trapped through the day in bright sunlight that they would surely normally shun, and hoped they too were for the same purpose and might be released soon.

San had had the perfect location in mind for the sunset. Burma is located sufficiently close to the equator for the sun set to occur within a short space of time. Soon the spectacular display of red, orange and mauve hues was over, and with the sun sinking out of sight into the mist on the horizon it was time to return to the ship. Again *Road to Mandalay* provided an excellent spot for a pre-dinner drink and an excellent dinner too. After dinner we found we had local performers to entertain us in the inside lounge. It was a low key affair and those on stage seemed somewhat inexperienced and shy; certainly the dancing did not have the extreme grace seen in traditional Thai dancing or the verve of Thai dances involving mock sword fights and clashing wooden staves. Nevertheless it was rather appealing and we had a number of performances ranging from traditional story telling dances to acrobatics. I will not forget the sight of a very slight young girl balancing on two bottles standing neck to neck, and in turn balanced on a stool, and keeping a cane ball aloft with her feet. She was clad in traditional costume, but wore bright socks with the woven name Nike on them. I wondered at what stage of her probably rudimentary education she had said to herself, "I think I'll be a bottle-balancing-ball-spinner"- maybe when she was not doing that she had other work too, though she must have done it regularly to keep in practice.

Also during the evening an astrologer and fortune teller visited the ship and a number of passengers, myself included, made appointments to see him for a consultation. I booked in for 6.30p.m. so that I could see him before dinner and eat with my future safely mapped out. But I felt that the need to make a booking was hardly a good sign. If he was any good shouldn't he have known when people were going to come and see him? When I did see him he took one look at me and delivered a veritable barrage of good news. Amongst the highlights I was evidently going to live virtually for ever. On the way I was definitely about to win the lottery, sell a million copies of my book and discover that Julia Roberts not only knew of me, but also could not wait to travel to England and meet me. Sadly this was not what actually occurred, though what he had to say was interesting, and besides don't you have to buy a ticket to win the lottery? Lillian had a session with him after dinner and later I asked how that had been. Her future looked good, she had been told, and she was already enthusiastically linking the prospect of a predicted financial windfall with an ability to finance future travels. The only snag was that good fortune appeared to depend on her getting rid of her much-loved cat. This presented something of a quandary and, while the outlook for her was good, similar good fortune may not have been in store for the cat. I have occasionally wondered since if a sign went up in her local shopping street: "Nice cat needs good home while owner has good fortune."

As the main part of the trip moved towards a close, there was only one disappointment, apart from not being able to stay longer, and that was that the visit had not coincided with the date of any major festival. The Burmese, in common with many Asian peoples, love a good festival. While these may well have serious purpose people do not let that get in the way of having a good time. For example, here the New Year is in March/April, the precise date varying rather as does Easter, except that here astrologers are the final arbiters of such matters. Festivities last several days and, while pagodas must be visited, feasts prepared and eaten and street parades watched or participated in, this particular event is characterised by an orgy of water throwing. Everything from pots and pails to hose pipes are brought to bear, and blessings for the coming year are conjured up by getting wet and soaking others. It is lucky the weather is so warm and drying off is no problem. No quarter is given and an unwary tourist will get as wet as everyone else. Given the importance of the occasion, *nats* are involved too as these are regarded as having a powerful effect on future prosperity. Water plays a part in other festivals too. In the full-moon festival of Kason, held a month or so after New Year, and in the rainy season, this too is a time for boat races and other water-borne spectaculars.

The Buddhist Lent starts at the full moon in June/July time and, despite the fact that many monks cut back on the frivolity and enter retreats, this is certainly a time of celebration. When Lent ends with the full moon of September/October the Festival of Light is held. Called Thadingkyut (Thadin means Lent and Kyut means end) it is a time when candles are lit in their millions and every house and public building is illuminated by their spluttering flames. This is done in memory of the time Buddha paid homage to his mother, Maidaw Maya, soon after his enlightenment, and people lit candles, lanterns and offered alms. Nowadays one element of the celebrations consists of families gathering together and children paying respect to their parents and giving them small gifts. The parents repay this gesture by offering good advice and maybe small amounts of money. Well just imagine! I cannot see this catching on at home, where too many parents have a job to give their children any advice at all and, at worst, get little from them by way of respect. Powerful traditional values are just one thing that gives Burma its unique character.

A final dinner and one last night sleeping aboard was all that remained before we moved on; *Road to Mandalay* continued to deliver its unique brand of top notch service, while creating a friendly and relaxed atmosphere at the same time.

*

On the far side of the airport lounge two doors stood side by side. One was labelled "Passport Control" and the other "Oversize". After several days of the *Road to Mandalay's* almost compulsory overindulgence I reckoned the choice for me was obvious. We had risen early on our last morning to catch the flight back to Yangon at a time that would give us some time in the city before travelling on to Bangkok in the evening. All these early mornings: we would definitely need a rest soon. Cases had to be collected at 6.00a.m. to be whisked ashore on the tender and we would not see them again until we arrived in Bangkok. Breakfast was a must and it was worth getting up just a little earlier than might otherwise have been necessary to give it time. Lillian, who had rushed off from dinner for her cat-threatening appointment with the fortune teller, asked if the dessert she had missed the night before could be amongst her breakfast choices. I think she said it jokingly, but it seemed to be a tribute to the anything-you-want service provided on the ship that such a request caused not a single eyebrow to lift even a millimetre and it was duly delivered with as much panache as everything else.

Joking or not originally, she expressed delight and tucked into it with gusto.

Various representatives of the crew were at the gangway to see us off. They had a new batch of passengers to cope with every week, but they bid us goodbye like old friends and, given the good time had by all, received many a thank you as people left the ship. For the last time, we climbed up the steep steps onto the path and clambered into the trusty bus. San, in charge of tickets, luggage and people, would accompany us to the airport and see us safely on our way. Mandalay had a new airport opened not long ago. On arrival we had of course come by ship, and now we would fly out and get a look at this on the way. First we had a drive of maybe 30 minutes. I expected this to be along the road we had arrived on, but soon we were winding through villages, passing inches from slow moving bullock carts and watching people getting to grips with the day and their daily routine. San explained that he had asked the driver to take "the pretty route". It was a good decision. Inevitably the sights of sounds of any travel experience fade to some extent with time, but the last things you do see may stick in the mind to a greater extent than other things. The images of people and of the dusty streets were powerfully characteristic of much of what we had seen around Mandalay. At one point a narrow road out of a village formed a long, straight stretch, walled on either side and with rows of trees in stately regularly spaced rows just beyond the walls. The road itself was rough, but it made an imposing route. "Lane for Kings" said San. There had to be a pagoda somewhere near. Our journey took a little longer than a direct route might have done, but was much better than going along the main road; when we did emerge onto a dual carriage way road, the surface of which was still very much third world, we were almost at the airport.

Getting through airports is not my favourite thing. Even a small one can be chaotic and difficult, and my one phobia is that I hate crowds. On this sort of trip having a guide and everything done for you was a real treat. We emerged from the bus, walked a few yards into the airport's outer hall and waited just a few minutes. Seemingly impossibly quickly San dispatched his assistant "K", who had been waiting at the airport to greet us, to the desks. In moments he was with us again, handing over boarding passes and San was wishing us a good journey. He had been an exemplary guide, patient, yet intent on making sure that we got everything possible from our visit. His enthusiasm was boundless, and his depth of information and knowledge was apparently infinite. He had not said as much, but it seemed clear from his manner that he saw himself as an ambassador for his country and felt passionately that people from outside should know about it. Whatever the standard of other things you experience when you aim to travel in some style, a trip can be made or broken by people. In this case San was an ideal guide. He made a wonderful experience exceptional. Of course, San's job depended on tourism, but I left him feeling that not only this suggested he was in favour of people visiting Burma. I felt he really felt that the country's history, culture and sights deserved to be widely experienced, that seeing it and learning something about it would enrich people's lives and that the Burmese people with whom visitors crossed paths benefited too. Certainly the way he went about his job gave this impression very strongly.

As a final gesture, he kindly would not hear of my going through the "Outsize" door and sent us off airside through the correct gate, watched our hand luggage being x-rayed and waited until we had disappeared into the lounge. This was a step or two up from what we had experienced on leaving Yangon, and we found a reasonably sized and modern Asian style room in which to wait. There was a small, rather unappealing, café counter. It was busy, but reasonably well organised, and we chatted to some of our fellow ship travellers now we were all going our separate ways, some straight home, others, like us, with a little more to do to complete our trip. It was clear that Burma had made a life enhancing impression on us all, even the most widely travelled amongst the passengers found it a new and wonderful experience. Soon it was time to board and we went down a modern escalator to the gate and took the inevitable bus to the plane.

This time an announcement had invited us to take advantage of "our free seating arrangement". This is what the British budget airlines go in for and it is a euphemism for a chaotic and unseemly scrum. In Britain it means no one is allocated a seat number and this seems to create a sort of herd instinct amongst airline passengers with a boarding pass with no seat number; when the gates are opened they surge forward as if as one. Any pushing and shoving is ignored by the check in staff, who wear smug expressions – they only smile if they spot someone whose luggage is too big or heavy so that they can take it away, put it in the hold and levy them a surcharge – and take a firm step back. This unruly queue will then hit the bottleneck of the entrance to the plane. Here the frustrations intensify and the weak and frail risk being trampled underfoot before they finally reach the comparative safety of a seat, usually to find it is too late to sit together with whomever they are travelling. Here we had the additional hazard of buses to contend with, but never the less, by some miracle we found ourselves at the front of the queue getting off the bus and got seats conveniently near the exit. Whatever scrum the arrangement had created was mainly lost behind us.

The plane repeated the crab-like takeoff of our journey from Yangon. Amazingly it took off a full fifteen minutes early. Whatever else you might say about this airline that was good, except presumably for any passenger arriving apparently right on time and finding they were left standing in the terminal. There were some empty seats so it was certainly possible that was exactly what had happened. What was said to any passengers left behind, I wonder? "Didn't we do well?" perhaps or maybe they gave the usual all-purpose excuse that it was due to "operational difficulties". This is a phrase universally used by airlines that covers everything from the pilot being held up on the way to the airport to an air hostess with a broken fingernail. During takeoff my wife again kept us safe by crushing my hand to a pulp and soon the short flight was over and announcements were being made about landing. It is said that a split second is defined as the tiny amount of time between the traffic light in front of you turning green and the driver behind you sounding their horn. So too there must be the tiniest measure of difference between a landing that gets you down safely and one that is hard enough to burst all the tyres on the landing gear, and get your picture in the morning newspaper alongside a fire engine, an ambulance and an airline representative trying to put a positive spin on the description "nearly crashed". We were just, by the narrowest of margins, into the category of safely down. But there was one hell of a bump, at least as many appalled gasps as on the landing in Bagan, and our teeth were still rattling as we walked into the terminal.

Driving to our hotel we saw, for the first time, a large number of police. There had only been one that we saw in the terminal and he was cosily and unthreateningly ensconced behind a desk reading a newspaper. Maybe he was involved in censorship and wanted to see how it had turned out. At one point along the road, however, we saw some twenty police and their various vehicles spread along about a hundred metres of road. Our driver told us we were passing the home of a senior member of the government. The fact that we otherwise saw very few policemen was explained to me as because the junta was so feared that no overt police presence was necessary. They are there soon enough when anyone transgresses in some way, and one can imagine that the definition of happiness in Burma is the feeling you get when there is a knock on the door after midnight, but when the policeman says a name you are able to tell him that he has the wrong address.

We had a room at the Dusit Hotel. Dusit is a Thai hotel chain with properties around the country. They have numbers of properties including a very good hotel in central Bangkok and another, which I have stayed at, on the island of Phuket: the Dusit Laguna. This was some years back when a Hong Kong company, for which I did some work, took me there along with a group of their staff from around the region. Most business travel is pretty dull, but this was unashamedly a pleasant place to go, well to be paid to go actually, and my wife was not thrilled about it as she was staying at home. She was even less pleased when the work went well and I returned with a second visit to the same hotel already in the diary. The signs here were just like other Dusits, a characteristic name in gold letters outside, but the Group ran this place in some sort of local partnership, an arrangement that I was told included the government. The brochure made it look splendid, and described it with curious phraseology as "... simply the last word in classic, sumptuously decorated with traditional Burmese teak furniture and flooring". It was in a great location looking out across Inya lake, but the rooms and the service were not as they would have been in Thailand. The photograph in the brochure of the bedroom proved to have been taken many years ago. In reality the place was a little old and tired, rather like I feel after a long haul flight. One thing that amused me was a sign on the reception desk that read: "We do not accept old, dirty or torn currency notes due to a regulation by Myanmar Investment Commercial Bank." They meant it too and every little transaction we had there, tea when we arrived, lunch and so on, resulted in each and every note I handed over being subjected to a slow and painstaking examination. My wallet seemed to contain a number that were pronounced as past their sell-by date and which were thus summarily rejected. Just what was going on here I have no idea. What sort of bank issues currency and then does its best to stop people using it? Or maybe it was the hotel. But why? It was not as if the notes could not be used elsewhere, ones in similar condition were snapped up by any market trader or shop one approached. Maybe someone did not want to get their hands dirty. As overall the hotel seemed a little run down, perhaps a little less time spent checking bank notes and a little more cleaning up and training staff might be a good idea.

It was, however, a good base from which to spend a little more time in Yangon and it was also only about ten minutes in a taxi from the downtown area. We used up the last of our spare Burmese currency buying two new dressing gowns, because, well, buying one each was guaranteed to get us a good deal. Even the scruffiest note was snapped up without any sort of protest. I am not a great one for souvenirs, but these were much overdue replacements and have proved excellent. I can now think of Burma in the bathroom almost every day.

Chapter Twelve

Chapter Thirteen

A HIGHFLYING SPOIL

"One of the pleasantest things in the world
is going on a long journey."
William Haslitt

Our flight from Yangon to Bangkok was uneventful. Ahead of this we discovered, somewhat belatedly, that Thai Airways did have an Executive Lounge in the terminal, hidden away at one end of the waiting area. It was small and busy with people but, as always, so much better than being with the herd. There were free refreshments and comfortable chairs and the television in the corner was showing an old James Bond film of the Roger Moore vintage. When it was time to go aboard, the bus was but a step away and boarding took place in an organised and civilised fashion. It was a relief to be in a large Thai Airways jet again and for the landing later on in Bangkok to be smooth as silk just as the airline's slogan says. This time I landed with my hand in good working order.

After a delightful time in Burma, Bangkok's Oriental Hotel again welcomed us. After all the early starts we had had over the last few days, it was good to have a lie in, so the next day started with a late breakfast on the terrace. I went ahead, found a table and settled down with a newspaper and an orange juice as I waited for my tea to arrive and my wife to catch me up. Almost at once I remembered I had left something in the room and went over to the nearest service station to ask if I could use a telephone. There was a telephone behind the desk, but another was quickly produced, a wire-free one I could take back to the table so that I could make the call comfortably from there. Nothing is too much trouble here and anything that will help a guest in some way, large or small, is considered the norm and delivered with maximum efficiency, minimum fuss and a certain indefinable but very real elegance. Breakfast was again a buffet arrangement on the terrace, but a certain amount is served and today my waitress was labelled "Trainee". Her status did not show in the service she provided, though it was apparent that she had a minder: one of the older waiters was shadowing her though usually at a discrete distance. He caught my eye and approached. "Everything okay?" he asked and I assured him it was. "We have to show her practical, theory not enough," he added by way of explanation out of her hearing. It surely worked. A leisurely breakfast is always a treat, and at the Oriental it is a joy.

After being in a technological black hole for a few days my next job was to catch up with the outside world and that meant checking my email. I do not have a Blackberry. I am not, I like to think, (too) obsessive about keeping in touch and had hardly mentioned the impossibility of being able to check my email over the last few days more than occasionally. Though in part, I must admit, this was because I knew it would make no difference. But now it had become important to catch up so I headed off to do just that.

In the Business Centre I found that many of my emails were routine, a few were more important and I spent a little while updating myself. One thing any sort of gap in checking email reminds you of is the horrendously pervasive nature of spam messages. It is a modern plague. With no checks possible for a few days I had many hundreds of them: a gallimaufry of admonishments all intent on parting me from my money, they had mostly been shunted into my junk mailbox. Who replies to such things? I receive enough dire warnings from friends more computer literate than I and in the media that such may well carry gazillions of viruses, worms and other sundry problem makers designed to send your computer into premature meltdown, to know to give them a wide berth. Yet one presumes they must bring some sort of response to their originators for them to bother sending them out at all. If I ever do want to contact an on-line gambling site, buy dubious medicines or contact a "sexy 24 year-old girl just waiting for your call," then I will find some other way of doing it. Sometimes I make a quick check of the messages in the spam folder as just occasionally real messages are shunted into it by mistake, but hey, I was on holiday, so I just deleted everything at a stroke, well at a click, and logged off.

Email updated, I sought out my wife by the swimming pool. She was sitting in a cabana, a two-person seat, probably six foot square and covered in towels and cushions with an awning set above it to provide shade. Near her was a large ceramic pot filled with water, one of many that are part of the hotel's attractive décor. Alongside it a member of staff was painstakingly preparing white lotus flowers, peeling off the outer covering and opening them up, so that they would float on the surface of the water. This is something you see around Asia; they look lovely, but I had never realised how much time and effort went into preparing them. Back in the room I found that I had apparently lost a pair of shoes. As I looked around I thought I heard a mobile phone ringing, it was muffled but appeared to be coming from inside the safe, which was in a wardrobe by the door. Baffled, I was just on the point of opening the safe when there was a knock at the door. It was Wirat the butler, and the pager at his waist was buzzing; the sound had not been from the safe but from outside the door. He stopped its noise and handed me a white draw-string bag. He cleared his throat: "I couldn't help seeing the tatty shoes you were wearing. We really can't have such things lowering the tone of this kind of establishment, so I gave them a good clean. They are still a bit rough, but you will at least look a bit more presentable now." No, of course he did not say that. I cannot now remember his exact words, but he was tact personified and he made the opportunity of cleaning up my appearance sound as if it had made his day. But maybe he *thought* what I imagined him saying, so I thought I would find him something else to do.

Earlier, my wife had been flicking through the stack of magazines that were in every room, mostly travel journals of some sort, and had suddenly shouted out. On one page was a feature about books and one of the items was a review of one of my books (*First class at last!*); a positive review too, dare I say, and a colour picture of the book's cover. So I asked Wirat if he could find me any more copies of the magazine, as I wanted to send the item to one or two people back home and the colour page would be more impressive than a photocopy. He promised to have a search and before we left he had successfully located several copies for me. I thanked him and, not for the first time, pondered how useful it would be to have such a person on hand at home.

Next we went shopping. Not my favourite thing, but as my wife said, "You don't think about presents" and insisted it was necessary. Bangkok now boasts shopping centres that are as glitzy as anything elsewhere in the world. At Paragon in Siam Square you can walk into the shopping centre direct from the Skytrain station and buy almost anything up to and including a Ferrari, who have a showroom high up in the tower along with a number of other prestige car manufacturers. This was not a major excursion. The Oriental have three hump-backed junk-style ferry boats, one goes to and fro to the nearest Skytrain station, from where many parts of the city are easily accessed. Another goes to and from their spa, which is across the river, and the third goes to a nearby shopping centre and pier, called River City.

Perhaps I should mention the Oriental's spa. If you follow in my footsteps, visit the Oriental and want to be pampered with a capital P, then this is for you, and because it is across the river you just might miss it. It offers a variety of treatments such as Oriental Body Wrap and Papaya Body Polish, and whole programmes of treatment with names like Eastern Delights and The Rejuvenator. You can evidently get through whatever constitutes Eastern Delights pretty quickly as it takes three hours, whereas The Rejuvenator is clearly more elaborate and is spread over three days. Draw your own conclusions about this time differential. I think I would expect to be pretty much reborn after three whole days of treatment, not just simply rejuvenated. The spa is a beautifully appointed Thai-style wooden building. One entrance takes you into a very traditional restaurant. Here, in a sumptuous room, low tables are ranged round foot wells to allow you to sit comfortably. Lunch is a buffet style meal and the evening meal is a la carte and is accompanied by a show consisting of Thai dancing and music. The menu is Thai.

Beyond the restaurant is the spa itself. Although I had neither time nor inclination for a treatment, I was welcomed in and given the grand tour. A number of treatment rooms were ranged over three floors connected by an imposing polished teak staircase. All the wood, especially the floors and staircase shone with evidence of assiduous polishing. If the massages offered were half as thorough then patrons would be buffed to within an inch of their lives. To say the treatment rooms were well equipped is a wholly inadequate description. They were large and clearly designed to spoil in a big, big way. A typical one had two treatment tables, a heat cabinet, a bath, a shower, loo and space for a whole army of people to minister to your needs. Some people check in and spend the whole day here; indeed, like the Rejuvenation deal, there are three-day packages that still manage not to repeat any of the many treatments that they offer during that time. If staying in this hotel is expensive, then staying for three days of treatment demands serious wealth, or a bank manager with the sort of forgiving nature that is rare these days when you get charged a ridiculous sum every time your bank sends you a letter.

Two particular things struck me about the place as a beautiful bare-footed Thai lady showed me round. First, one of the two kinds of treatment table was of teak wood. Not very comfortable looking, but designed to facilitate massages involving scented oils. These had a drain hole to steer any excess oil safely into some suitable hideaway. Despite the setting I could not shake off the vision of a mortuary these conjured up. They somehow looked best suited to dead bodies, and I just hoped that *Can you massage my right leg next* did not sound anything like the Thai words for *Please start the autopsy now*. Perhaps I've been watching too much television, no stainless steel saws were in evidence, but there were a variety of cabinets and unmarked drawers. My guide smiled sweetly and this reassured me; she did not look anything like the chief dismemberer. Secondly, I noticed that half the treatment rooms were doubles. They had extra large baths and two-by-two treatment tables. I commented on this and was told, "Oh yes, double very sensuous". I'm sure, and in these hedonistic days I can well believe it. Even so, I found it difficult to imagine. Just how did they combine the sensuous bit with the treatment? Would their customers not find that having a face pack applied just as their libido went into overdrive was, well, just the tiniest bit off-putting? And what about those administering the treatments? I cannot imagine that at such an illustrious establishment they were available to join in. Perhaps they were just practiced in knowing when to make a strategic withdrawal; or perhaps that was sometimes what the customers had to do just as the face pack descended. I found myself unable to conjure up a suitable question to cast more light on all of this without leading to terminal embarrassment or running the risk of harassment charges, so I left it there. I still wonder, now I can think about it again, precisely how it works. Sadly, a visit is sufficiently expensive to protect me from the truth. I left in ignorance. My guide had offered no addition to her "sensuous" comment; nor did she stop smiling.

We landed at River City just at the wrong moment. From the pier here a number of river cruises depart. These are fair sized boats and every hotel in the city has a desk selling tours.

Such cruises are always featured and they are a popular choice for many visitors with little time in the city and who, from my single experience, are not over fussy about the quality of their food. To cruise along a river, particularly one offering so much to see as this, as you eat is certainly pleasant. But in a city offering such a plethora of great eating experiences, a poor one is a real disappointment. The jetty was full of people, some just waiting for their particular boat to arrive, others actually making their way to one already moored and waiting to load up and go. Now "making their way" is not really the way to put it. They behaved as if somewhere behind them there was a herd of charging elephants and they had been given instructions to move it or be trampled to death underfoot. They swept everything in their path aside, including us. There were a variety of nationalities represented, all as rude and selfish as each other. There was a momentary hiatus as we and others disembarking from our and other boats tried to go against the tide during which I rehearsed various things to say: *Get off my foot you lout... Don't bloody push...* or just: *Stop... Help...* or: *There are no elephants!* In the end I said nothing. We battled our way through diagonally and were able to get around the queue from behind. Phew - some people! I wonder if they are always like that or if it is behaviour brought on by being far from home, the heat or being in a crowd; or all three. Whatever the reason it made a budget airlines free seating scrum seem almost civilised.

After a moment inside the air-conditioned open lobby of River City to regain our equilibrium, I had a wander round while my wife went to buy presents. She would be a while, I knew, and on previous occasions she has spent so long in a shop I have filed a missing persons report with the police. In Thailand shopping can be fun. You have to find what you want, you may well be concerned to negotiate a good price, a process which can go on some time and is certainly fun, but it is an experience too as people are so friendly. They want your business, they love it when you come back, but they love to chat too: my wife spent three quarters of an hour in one small shop because, as she said, "... the woman running it was so nice". I toured the upper floors where the shops mainly sell antiques. Things there are expensive, usually from my standpoint prohibitively so, but it is intriguing to look and besides doing so protected me from the protracted thinking process that I find seems to precede my wife buying the simplest item as she weighs up what is best. She does it well I know, (very well, if you are reading this) but it does take *so long*. On another occasion in Thailand while I waited as she pondered a number of purchases, the woman shop owner joked with me about it and I referred to my wife as a "big problem" (only in the shopping sense, of course). She replied quickly, "That's not a big problem, just a woman."

One thing that makes for good presents is the many items made in Thai silk. The quality of this rich fabric is rightly famous around the world.

Silk is another of those things apt to be taken for granted; its production overlooked as you simply focus on the quality of it as it is offered in the shops. Silk production goes back to almost 3000 years BC and it is uncertain whether China or Thailand made it first. Its manufacture in Thailand received a great boost when the American Jim Thomson set up his business in Thailand in the 1940s; he later disappeared in mysterious circumstances on a morning walk in Malaysia, never to be seen again and with his disappearance never explained. His business lives on, with shops around Thailand and elsewhere and his house now an appealing museum giving a fascinating glimpse at life in Thailand in days gone by.

Silk is a natural product. The silkworm moths, from which it comes, live only about four days, but lay thousands of eggs, the worms that hatch from them eat nothing but mulberry tree leaves and are protected and kept on trays while they grow. After a month or so during which they increase their weight 1,000 times, they spin cocoons.

Once production starts the cocoons are put in water at about 80 degrees, which releases the silk threads. These are lifted out of the water with a forked bamboo stick and laid to and fro across a tray while being regularly sprinkled with rice to dry them. From there they are then reeled onto a spool. The raw silk is rough, and it is soaked in soapy water to soften it; it is coated with a sticky substance called sericin, which must be removed; that done it can then be dyed. The best silk uses natural dyes from various plants and bark. Sometimes the thread will be tie-dyed to create a pattern: *mud mee* silk. Silk fabric is then woven on upright looms worked by a foot pedal. The process is lengthy and exacting, although much of it is mechanised nowadays, and some silk is mixed with polyester to make it cheaper and easier to wash. But it remains a classic fabric and the best of it, with its geometric patterns and profusion of bright and subtle colours make whatever it is used for display real class. That little worm must have aided many a seduction too. Stockings and lingerie have an allure far removed from a creepy crawly and many a romantic novel would not be the same without a line such as that immortalised by Peter Sellers in the days he made old fashioned records: *he ripped the thin silk from her...*

*

With presents successfully bought we met up and ate supper in a small restaurant overlooking the river. The dinner cruise boats go first up river, then retrace their steps and go back in the other direction and on down river. As we ate we saw more than one of them go by on its second leg. By the time we headed back the jetty was deserted and we were whisked back to the Oriental's pier in style. This time we were the only passengers on the smart ferry and it seemed almost like having a private boat.

Wonderful though the Oriental was, and one could laze by its pool watching the busy river for a long time, we were in a city with a plethora of culture and history and making a more cultural excursion seemed only right. Some of the main sights, certainly the easiest to access, are along the river: The Grand Palace, The Royal Barges and more. If you go anywhere at all in Bangkok the first thing to consider is how you get there. An ill-judged journey that maroons you interminably in Bangkok's notorious traffic is guaranteed not to make you fall in love with the place. Having seen most of the main sights at one time or another, we decided to compromise and visit Vimanmek Mansion. A discussion at the concierge desk had produced a shoal of leaflets, carefully considered advice and some notes written in Thai to help us ensure that a taxi took us where we wanted to go and not on an ad hoc tour of dubious jewellery outlets. A short phrase - "Must look, only five minutes" – from a Thai taxi driver responded to injudiciously can see an entire morning disappear as they whisk you away in the hope of earning some commission on your visit to a jewellery or silk emporium. From where we were, Vimanmek could be reached by getting a boat along the river to a spot a few piers further along beyond the Grand Palace. Then taking a taxi for only a manageable distance would complete the journey to the Mansion. When you first visit a city, sightseeing is usually a priority, once you have been a few times, you settle into a different routine, you know where you like to stay and are apt to settle for visiting a favourite restaurant rather than another museum. I was conscious that this approach had left me with a good deal more to see in Bangkok and this particular place, a mansion surrounded by other buildings and the Royal Elephant National Museum, was recommended. It was guaranteed to be first class and not the least bit scary. I never tire of river trips, and this one took about 25 minutes and gave ample opportunity to watch the world go by.

On the way our boatman, who was actually a woman, manoeuvred to a halt alongside another boat coming down the river. She had apparently spotted this at some distance. It had another woman "driver" and they engaged in a brief chat and our lady collected her lunch from her friend in a wicker basket. If I understood her explanation correctly, they took turns to prepare food, then had to make sure their different journeys up and down the river coincided so that one did not go hungry. Back on shore we found a taxi and the note we had brought from the hotel worked well. Soon we were pulling into to the grounds and walking to the Mansion.

We paid the minimal entry fee - such things are really inexpensive here - walked up the steps to the imposing entrance and had to wait five minutes for the next English language tour. You cannot walk round alone here, so information comes as part of the deal. Vimanmek Mansion is reputed to be the largest teakwood mansion in the world. It consists of two three-story, red-tiled wings set at right angles, with a four-story octagonal section at one end. It has a curious history. From 1906 to 1910 when he died, King Rama V lived in Chitrlada Palace. Ahead of this being completed he needed somewhere else to live for a while and arranged for the Munthatu Rattanaroj Residence in Chuthathuj Rachathan at Koh Sri Chang in Chonburi to be dismantled and brought to Bangkok. It must have set someone a few problems as it is a building of considerable size, but what the King wanted no doubt the King got. So it was re-erected in Dusit Gardens in 1901, this being an area of orchards and paddy fields, which the King had bought earlier, in 1897, and had laid out as gardens. The cost of so doing does not seem to be recorded. He then lived there for five years until his new home was ready. Curiously during this time, apart from the king and his family only women were allowed in the Palace. For a while thereafter the Mansion was kept up well. Queen Consort Indharasaksaji lived there for a while after the King moved, but she moved on following the King's death, with the Mansion then being used only as a storage place for items surplus to Royal requirements. Most of us make do with a loft or box room for such things, but royalty are evidently able to store their junk in much greater style. That done it went right out of the Royal minds.

Only in 1982 did Queen Sirikit rediscover the place and, with the current King's blessing, arranged for it to be renovated and become a museum so as to commemorate King Rama V by displaying his personal photographs, art and handicraft items. She saw it as a showcase of Thai heritage, open for all to see and view its collection of silverware, ceramics, crystal ware, ivory, pictures and artefacts from around the world. Other items are displayed there too, and such include an old manual typewriter, the first machine to use the Thai alphabet. Why? It just happened to need a home at the time, I guess.

Our guide arrived, a lady dressed in a plain, almost military-style uniform, and we joined a group of perhaps a dozen English speakers on the next tour. It was a fascinating place. First, in terms of the individual items displayed, much of it, like tableware from England and France, from overseas, and secondly as a building. In my experience, so many such places have been set up as museums in a way that makes it difficult to imagine them in use: in this case as a home. As we walked along the corridor that ran round much of the outer edge of the building, once an open veranda to protect the rooms from the sun and heat, the sensitively made arrangements here were such that it was very easy to imagine life going on when it was a palace. The rooms we were shown through still looked much as they must have done when the Mansion was occupied. There was a music room, an audience chamber and other public rooms as well as the Royal apartments, which were housed in the octagonal part of the building. All was set out pretty much as it used to be, right down to the King's bathroom, though he seemed to have taken his toothbrush away with him. The wooden building itself was impressive, and was constructed entirely without nails using only wooden pegs to pin the timber together. Presumably this also helped make it possible to dismantle the building in order to transport it across the country to its present home. In look it has an elaborate, western influenced style. The teak floors showed the result of regular polishing over many years. They had a rich sheen that looked as smooth as a mirror, and everywhere the view outside was of beautiful gardens. In the early nineteen hundreds this must have been a tranquil spot. The sights and sounds of life going on in it could easily be conjured up. Few such places really allow you to imagine them as they were; the way Vimanmek Mansion is now presented has been well thought out. It works and goes comfortably on my list of places to visit in Bangkok that I can unhesitatingly recommend.

We returned to the hotel sad to be taking our leave of it. But there was one more treat to come.

Chapter Thirteen

Chapter Fourteen

NOW FOR A REST

"Like all great travellers, I have seen more than I remember, and remember more than I have seen."
Benjamin Disraeli

The Oriental Hotel is a one-off. Why ever you might stay there, whether it is for the efficiencies it brings to an important business visit or, as in our case, just for the sheer joy of it, it is special. An Englishman staying on our floor exchanged some words with me in the elevator and when asked about the hotel, said simply, "There is nowhere else I would stay in this city." How the other half lives. But even for ordinary mortals as a one-off special treat, it is not to be missed. We could stay no longer, however, but did not intend to return home yet either.

Instead we went to Koh Samui. The human mind has an almost infinite ability to rationalise things and justify itself, and nowhere is this truer than with regard to expenditure, and travel expenditure in particular. Let's go to India, or anywhere else for that matter, people say, followed immediately by reservations. It would be too expensive, it's a long flight and we would need to go for three weeks to make it worthwhile. But... and then the justifications start: we deserve a special break, we only took a short holiday last year, it would be educational for the children or, if you are older, we should do it while we can. Such thoughts become increasingly irrational as they are added to: after all, we ask, where else can you get such a good curry, ride an elephant or see the Taj Mahal?

So it was that we went to an island resort. Well, having flown so far it was obviously silly not to make the most of the cost. The Burma tour had been hectic and we deserved a rest; I could sit back and sort out my notes or do some writing; we had not been there for eighteen years and wanted to see how much it had changed. Damn it, hang the rationalising. It would just be nice – a luxury trip it had been so far but it would not be complete without a spell by the sea.

The Thai island of Koh Samui (Koh means island) is some 250 square kilometres in extent, making it the largest of Thailand's many islands. It first became known in the west as a backpacker destination. It was a place you visited if you wanted your journey to the East to have an exotic edge to it. It was pioneer territory where the sun shone, the beer was cheap and cold and the beautiful unspoilt beaches were virtually your own. I first went there in the late eighties. I was not a pioneer by that date, but it was still something of a jump into the unknown for me, one involving an overnight train journey out of Bangkok and a ferry from the mainland as this was before there was an airport on the island.

On that first occasion the train was busy, simple, but surprisingly civilised. It departed from Bangkok in the late evening, and bunks were soon folded out of the walls above the seats in the open carriages and people climbed up to sleep and drew the curtains behind them. All the locals seemed to be travelling with enormous volumes of luggage and were also well equipped for the journey; they did not quite light campfires in the aisle to cook their breakfast on, but they came pretty darned close.

The train connected with a ferry and we set off to the island, luggage and people cluttering the cramped open deck. My suitcase was wedged between a wooden crate full of live chickens and a large square package tightly wrapped in sacking. We had been told, and I had checked in numbers of ways, that finding accommodation was easy. Groups of beach bungalows were positioned around the island, some pretty primitive and others "really very nice". Occupancy was not high we were told, just choose the best. We asked a driver to take us to the beach we needed to be at and he did so, but could offer no advice as to where we could stay. "Everywhere full for New Year," he said. Naively perhaps my enquiries had neglected to mention to those who advised us that New Year's Eve was to occur in the middle of our stay.

Also naively we had arranged to meet a friend from Australia. A series of postcards (this was before email made such arrangements so much easier – and yes, young readers, there was a time when email was not routine, indeed one when it did not exist at all and life was actually – believe it or not – still possible) had set this up. Ad hoc it may have been, but we expected it to work. The intention was to meet at White House, then the island's only actual hotel, albeit a small one, and have a meal and a drink on the evening of December 31st to catch up and see in the New Year. We went to the hotel. Its rooms were all taken, of course. I left my wife guarding the luggage and walked along the beach from one clutch of bungalows to the next to try and find accommodation. All were fully booked. I found none free and returned to the hotel after a couple of hours with mild heat stroke, a dire need for water and little clue as to what to do next.

At this point the owners of the hotel, who were a Swiss man with a Thai wife, took pity on us. Some sort of juggling and doubling up of friends staying with them for New Year gave us a room at least until we could get into a bungalow after New Year's eve. This entire trauma was made much better when Di walked in a couple of hours before the New Year dawned. Travelling from opposite sides of the world our meeting plans had been successful. Di is a delight: my wife first met her on a holiday many years ago: she is the sort of person you can see rarely but pick up with when you do as if you had last spoken yesterday. It was a splendid reunion and we celebrated the New Year in style.

The second time I went to the island was soon after the airport opened. Suddenly it seemed that one could go somewhere exotic without any undue hassle. So, after the long haul flight from the U.K. my wife and I transferred to Bangkok airport's domestic terminal and went to check in for the onward flight. The desk was closed. Time passed and finally someone appeared, but only for the harassed looking clerk to post a notice saying, "Flight cancelled" on the counter top. A clutch of people was, like us, standing waiting and others now came forward to see what was going on. The notice poster began to walk away, and there were cries of, "Wait a minute!" and "What's going on?" He looked alarmed; his job had been to post the notice not to engage in communication with what looked like a potentially hostile group. He hesitated, but he turned back and stood behind the counter facing us. "Why is the flight cancelled?" someone asked. He explained that there had been a storm, adding encouragingly that a plane had been lost only weeks before in an earlier storm and that as a result restrictions in such circumstances had been tightened. Quite right too I thought. I had no wish to crash into a tropical ocean in the middle of a storm. "But what do we do now?" someone else asked. The answer was apparently simple: "No flight. No go," he said turning to leave. Some passengers, locals I guess, perhaps used to this sort of thing and with only a weekend to cancel, left to go home. A number of the group had, like us, a whole holiday in front of them. I pushed forward and asked "What alternative arrangement can you make?" and what proved to be a New Zealand voice next to me promptly added, "What about a coach?" Notice-poster sighed and moved back behind the counter. He had clearly been hoping to avoid all this, just to scuttle off to his back office and have a nice cup of tea perhaps. "A coach might be possible if numbers are right," he said and left it to us to do a rapid count – some thirty people needed transport. He sighed again and picked up the telephone. He talked at length in Thai. No one understood, though everyone hoped a resolution was in prospect; if not he might have a revolution on his hands. Finally he put the phone down and announced, "You have coach. In one hour". We waited. After that hour and two more had passed, it arrived, luggage was stowed beneath it and the weary passengers climbed aboard.

The coach was air-conditioned. Good. But bad too: the air-con had only two settings: on and freezing cold or off, in which case the temperature soared. Most passengers were not dressed for this; we had expected to transfer swiftly to another plane, indeed we should have been in our hotels long ago. We froze, we asked for the air-con to be switched off.

We boiled. We asked for it to be switched on again. Our driver was seemingly indifferent to our plight. He spoke, or professed to speak, no English, though he was educated to the on/off routine pretty quickly. We sat with the New Zealander Keith, who had also assisted in getting the alternative transport fixed, and his wife Nan. We had plenty of time to get to know them. The journey lasted fourteen interminable hours and became not just increasingly uncomfortable but akin to torture.

At one point, apparently by arrangement, we stopped at a café outside the small coastal town of Hua Hin. It was little more than a shack with an awning in front. We sat on small stools by the roadside, with traffic roaring past what seemed like a few inches away, and were given a very indifferent meal. This, together with a few other stops to stretch our legs and visit toilets of dubious cleanliness, but beloved by the insect population of the area, punctuated the long journey and finally we arrived on the coast at Surat Thani.

Finally, as we came towards the ferry port to make the crossing to the island, once we got within sight of the ferry the driver became locked in traffic. We would have missed the boat if we had not demanded access to our luggage and rushed, puffing and panting, the last couple of hundred metres to the gangway. We boarded the ferry with only a minute or two to spare; it was again a simple vessel and we sat on top on our suitcases. It was a choppy crossing, proof if proof was needed that there had been a storm here. We sat on deck for an hour, hoping the fresh air would curtail any feelings of sickness. When we beached on the island we clambered into *Baht* buses, pickup trucks with seats under an awning in the back charging just a few Thai *Baht* for journeys around the island. We headed off for our respective accommodation: us to the hotel, which had rescued us on our last visit, Keith and Nan to another small resort a little way away. As we arrived at The White House the skies opened, lightning flickered and the rain came down not so much as stair rods, rather broom handles. Maybe it was not a day to fly.

The holiday went well. One incident I remember especially clearly. We had arranged to meet up with our new New Zealand friends and hire a car together to tour the island. I was to arrange this, so I went to the hotel manager and made the arrangement: he said that a Suzuki jeep would be at the front door ready to go in the morning and indeed it was. I asked if there was anything to sign and was told "No need". "What about insurance?" I asked. A question: "Are you going to have an accident?" was the response, to which I said that I certainly did not intend to. "Okay, fill in the form when you get back if you have an accident," he said. "If not forget it and you will save some money." Maybe there was still a pioneering element to the place even in those days. We had a pleasant day out, filled up with petrol from a pump where the purchaser had to literally pump the handle to get the fuel flowing, there was no accident and the money saved just about covered the cost of dinner.

So, some of this had been a bit basic, but the island was lovely and I had always been determined to go back. Now, to create a suitable final stage of this journey, some first class time on the beach seemed an ideal way to round things off.

At Suvarnabhumi airport, the troubles with their new facilities continued. We arrived at check in only to be told, "Sorry, computers down, please come back in half an hour". We found a seat and after a little time, as other people began to appear I went up to ask again. They had clearly decided that the computers were not going to play ball at least in time for this flight and that we must all be checked in manually. The girl at the desk decided to make a start and having told me this went straight on to check us in. For once I was in just the right place at the right time. She painstakingly wrote all the necessary details in clear capital letters on our boarding cards. I would have hated to be at the back of the queue that was now forming behind us. Checking everyone in was going to take a while. We proceeded on without problem, spent a short time in Bangkok Airways lounge, sorry boutique lounge, whatever that means, and boarded the plane right on time. Last time when we visited Koh Samui but only flew back, the planes used had been quite small and propeller driven. This time it was a fair sized jet. It's only a short hop and across the water the whole way, though there was hardly time to play a game that I find passes the time on flights, and in which you imagine that you crash into the sea and are washed ashore on a desert island. Which of your fellow passengers do you save and which do you eat? In your daydream this is a choice that must be made on minimal information, after all you have probably not spoken to most of them. You can engage in flights of fancy or try to be practical, even well cooked that fat woman at the back would tax any plastic cutlery washed ashore with you, so perhaps it would be better to choose a more manageable meal. My nemesis Harold would certainly not be on my "to save" list.

We were soon landing at Koh Samui airport. When we had flown out after our last visit the airport had only one building, an open sided one with a thatched roof. We sped down the runway, alongside which was a sea of flowers, then disembarked into tiny, open sided buses, which the driver controlled with a handle as from an old-style mangle, which stuck up from the surface in front of him. It appeared to need a good spin to make a turn. Soon the ride was over.

The old building was still there, although it had been extended and others added around it. We waited for luggage alongside the most primitive carousal you can imagine. There had been no such thing on our last visit, but this seemed to suffice and in due course we saw an open luggage truck draw up and unload suitcases onto the moving surface. Before long we retrieved ours and as we stepped out a uniformed driver was walking in holding up a sign from Napasai with my name on it. We were soon in a large 4 x 4 being whisked away to the resort. Napasai is a smart fifty villa property, one of comparatively few on this now crowded island that can be called exclusive, and which is set distinctly apart from the hurly burly of activity that prevails along much of the coast.

This resort is a treat. In for a penny, in for a pound, we had decided to continue to do things in style for a final few days. The accommodation is spread over a hillside running down to a private beach. We had a balcony looking out across the sea, and a good sized bedroom and bathroom. As befits such a place the welcome was warm and efficient and the standard of the place obvious. The main building consists of a reception area and, a level down, a bar and lounge area looking across the gardens to the sea. We were taken down a winding path by Nit, from the reception area, and given a guided tour on the way: he pointed out the pool, two restaurants, and the bar by the beach and mentioned other things in the distance such as a gym and library. At one point a lizard a foot long, and with a tail to match, crossed the path in front of me and I, being from a country without such creatures, commented on its size. "Not big, small", said Nit and added "it will not bite," to reassure me in a way that suggested there had been previous ignorant guests who bolted at the sight. He then quickly moved smoothly on to describe whatever was next on our induction tour.

We spent a few quiet days doing very little. Nothing to fear here it seemed, now we knew that the lizards didn't bite. Having found my fears about Burma largely unfounded, we woke up one morning to find that there had been an earthquake there. No wonder the pagodas in Burma had suffered so much damage over the years. This one was located six miles deep in the earth on the Burma/Laos border just north of Thailand. It was of 6.3 magnitude and shook for more than thirty seconds. Its shock was noticeable over a wide area, and in several countries. There was some damage: in Chiang Rai for instance, the locus shaped top fell off a temple, Wat Pasak. Mostly damage was superficial, although it was described as the largest earthquake ever recorded in northern Thailand. In Bangkok, where earthquakes are rarely noticed, this time in was sufficiently severe for the newspapers to report that some people rushed out of offices into Silom Road to see what was going on. As Pat Pong, the bar and red light area, is nearby maybe the earth really did move for some people. In Koh Samui it went unnoticed by everyone except those with seismic detectors in their living rooms.

We ventured out once to see what had become of the place where we had stayed in the past. We went first to a nearby fishing village, then to Chaweng Beach. In both cases the roads were now a solid, untidy line of shops, cafes, guest houses and there was a distinctly international feel to the streets with names such as Starbucks and McDonalds emblazoned above modern concrete and steel frontages set amongst the simpler buildings. It was all tourist orientated: many cafes advertised "English Breakfast", every fourth shop offered Internet access and "Cheap international calls", the bars offered international brands of beer and although the people offering all this were Thai, in many ways there was precious little feeling of Thailand about it. There was a surfeit of tailors. Most seemed to be run by Indians and they approached everyone, "How are you? Tailor for you? Let me give you my card", though few hot tourists in sweaty T-shirts were in the mood to buy a suit. Many people still have good holidays here I am sure and there are a variety of resorts to cater to all tastes, but of what we had experienced years ago there was little sign. It was sufficiently long ago for this to be unsurprising, I guess, but the extent of tourism linked building and development was still something of a shock.

In addition, Koh Samui, as many other places in Thailand, has become popular for those wanting to own a second home overseas and for those retiring and moving from countries such as England, Germany and Australia, so there are property shops and evidence of building everywhere. There are some great homes on offer and costs are certainly much less than in Europe, though it is not an easy place to buy without good advice and the legal requirements can be somewhat obscure and a trap for the unwary. Planning does not seem to be a word with a direct equivalent in Thai; certainly not as used elsewhere as in "planning restrictions". The advice of one local was to "never buy anything with a wonderful view that has any space in front of it to build something else. You may go away for a few months and then come back to find that your view is now the back wall of a condominium". I sometimes wish that I had invested in property in Thailand 20 years or so ago, when you could buy good beach front property for what now seems like a song. We had a good tour around, but went back to Napasai, the beach front of which might persuade you that you were in the only inhabited spot on the island, to think back to how it had been.

During our stay I had a word with the resort's manager, Franz Von Merhart. He was a French/German, had been brought up in Africa, trained in France and had worked in Asia for some time. He was responsible for opening this hotel and had run it for the three years since then. The name of the place is Napasai. It is not Napasai Hotel or Resort, and this is just one small sign of its exclusivity. Given what we had discovered round about, and the profusion of low cost accommodation, this is one of a proportionately small number of such resorts on the island. It claims to be the best and certainly it must be high on the list. Set along the beach, with accommodation primarily in four layers of villas on the hill back from the beach, all with a view across the sea towards Koh Phanang, a smaller island now busy developing itself and becoming much more "sophisticated", the place has both character and charm. It is a garden setting with coconut and cashew nut trees giving shade. Like most places in Thailand, large and small, its charm comes in large part from its staff. Franz told me that most of his time was spent with the team and that the idea was to create a situation in which they not only gave good service, but also engaged with guests and added to the atmosphere.

One example of this was that there were no signs around the hotel, none of the profusion of notices usual elsewhere saying, "Pool", "Restaurant", "Gym" and so on. "This is intentional," he told me. "We brief guests when they arrive and thereafter if they need directions they can ask and staff may be able to do more than just point the way." It worked too: I asked someone by the pool what the small number of local people were doing wading between the rocks on the beach at low tide. I was told that they caught squid, crabs and oysters and I think I could have got the full life history of individual fishermen if I had wanted. "Service and the right attitude comes first from a feeling of family," Franz told me. "We make sure that our people feel they belong and mix more experienced staff with any trainees so that everyone helps each other and everyone learns all the time." With different nationalities to deal with, sometimes coming primarily at specific times of the year, there were even briefings about how people differed and what to expect from them. "For example," he said, "We all need to appreciate that the Spanish, who come in large numbers in June, never want to eat until after ten o'clock in the evening." During such times the restaurants and their staff just had to change their routines a little, I guess. Certainly, I have nothing but praise for the service we received.

At one point during our chat he shooed away a cat. Cats can be a pest in this part of the world, but here there seemed only to be two or three, which I had imagined were tolerated in light of their chasing away less desirable creatures. It transpired that there was a long running contretemps between him and the assistant manager, a woman, who liked and looked after the cats. It was clearly long term, but Franz held out hopes of ultimate victory.

The only thing that really drove me mad during the stay was the computer on the lobby bar counter, which provided 24-hour free Internet access. First, it was not set at desk height so that anyone using had to reach up and operate the keyboard at an unnatural angle, and secondly various important keys did not function at all. It is surprisingly difficult to type and try to remember for instance that one shift key is not working and use the other one. In some ways such inconveniences are minor, but this was annoying – and soon to be replaced, I was reassured.

Under thatched roofs beyond the pool were the two seating areas of an outdoor bar. Fans turned in the roof to stir the humid air and it was an excellent place to relax in the early evening as you looked out across the sea with other islands visible in the distance. When the sun set over the sea in a blaze of colour this was the place to be. During our visit there were some monsoon downpours in the early evening that banished the sun. One of the staff told me that at this time of year, "It is cool in the early morning, very nice; then it is too hot, then it rains." Not every day though. On one dry evening I sat with a cold beer in front of me, and was listening to, alright eavesdropping on, a young French couple being briefed about the diving trip they were taking on the following day. It sounded good and the briefing was thorough: equipment, safety procedures, it was all there. My ears really pricked up at the mention of sharks, especially as these were apparently being mentioned as an attraction. It was not: "This is how we avoid coming within a thousand miles of a shark." It was more: "Lucky you, you have a good chance of seeing some reef sharks. Up close. Sorry they are not likely to be very large ones, only somewhere between one and two metres long." That must make their mouths big enough to ... no, I did not want to go there. Then further information was added. "There's no feeding of sharks here," said the instructor, "so they don't associate people with food." Well, there's a relief. Although surely the way this was explained meant that they would eat you if they realised you were tasty, but luckily it had not dawned on them. Well. Not. Yet. No wonder I've never dived. I would not want to be there on the day when their perception goes up a notch.

Then the following morning a sign went up at one end of the pool and a man began laying out diving equipment, flippers, air cylinders, masks and all, on the poolside. A free lesson was on offer. The pool here is lovely. It is a long infinity pool with a horizon edge facing the sea and an undulating edge on the other side. I had swum in it a number of times; I had swum some lengths mid morning as an intended antidote to the hotel's excellent, and irresistible, buffet breakfast and in a desperate attempt to maintain the status quo weight wise. I am as sure as I can possibly be that, at least while I was there, it never contained a single shark, reef or otherwise, and certainly nothing of the sort of size that I had heard being discussed on the previous evening.

So I had a go.

There was no queue forming yet as I introduced myself to Ian Klaczak, despite the name an Englishman who told me that his name went "way back". He was today's instructor in attendance, and he quickly began to explain what we would do. I would wear a weighted belt to make me sink. But the jacket in which the air tank was an integral part would balance this out; the intention was to achieve neutral buoyancy. I put on the belt and then the waistcoat style jacket. There were several pipes coming off it. One had the instruments on it that a real dive would necessitate: they indicated depth, and the amount of time left before the air ran out and you drowned. There was a third one too, though I can't remember what it was; without my spectacles they were all a blur anyway. In any apocalyptic movie, the kind which starts with a ragged band of people struggling out of a bunker after the bomb has dropped or the aliens have invaded, there is always a moment when one of these characters get his glasses broken. And instantly, as they peer helplessly around them, you know that they are doomed and won't be one of the ultimate survivors come the final reel. My eyesight is, it seems, similarly ill suited for diving. I was assured it did not matter here in the confines of the pool.

There were also two breathing nozzles, one in case of emergency, not least so that two divers could use one tank to get back to the surface if the equipment of one should fail. The emergency one was bright yellow. A button on these blew any water out and soon I had donned a face mask too and was being told to "breathe normally" as we lay face down in the shallow end of the pool. I thought breathing would be a much stranger process than, in fact, it was. The face mask covered my nose, fitted snugly, and the breathing tube in my mouth also felt secure. I just breathed in and out steadily, emitting a cloud of bubbles with the outward breath to reassure myself that life was continuing. Ian checked that I was doing everything correctly, and then he ran through some basic signals, because, as he explained patiently, "We won't be able to speak underwater". Right, good point. At this at least I was a fast learner, and soon we agreed that I knew how to signal for left, right, up and down and also to ask for help; the last surely the most important sign of all. He also showed me the signal for okay, made with the index finger forming a circle with the thumb; presumably this one needs some variants internationally, as there are a number of countries, including Brazil, where such a gesture is obscene.

Then we were off, and I was swimming along close to the bottom of the pool, right down its length to where it was about two metres deep at the deep end. The sensation was amazing. In two minutes underwater I was transformed into a secret agent going to defuse a mine and save the world. Scuba diving has always looked an attractive thing to do and now I knew it really must be. If I stopped moving I simply hung in the water, going neither up nor down. I felt like a seagull looks as it hangs effortlessly in the sea breeze. I had to imagine the wonders of the deep and doing this in the sea, in clear, though hopefully in my case shark-free, water; and indeed I could do so all too easily. When my turn finished I was hooked. I wanted to surface and simply say, "Where do I sign? When can I go out to sea? How long does it take to qualify?" But we were to leave the next morning, so any enthusiasm must wait for another occasion. Ian, who was perhaps 30 years old, worked for 100 Degrees East. He had learnt his diving in Egypt, given up work in an I.T. firm and now lived here permanently. "I don't earn as much money," he said, "but the cost of living is less here and I just love the lifestyle." He had graduated from simply being an instructor and now helped run the company. Still, I cannot imagine a better teacher: his manner was intelligent, clear and calm. Seek him out if you fancy lessons. And thank you Ian, you have made me add one more thing to the list of the hundred things I must do before I die, though can I stipulate the no-shark option please?

Only a couple of other people had a go, and a young Englishman on his honeymoon went next. I watched and was interested to see how I must have looked from above. Despite being on honeymoon, he seemed to have enough breath left and told me afterwards that he had enjoyed it very much: the diving that is; I did not pry about the honeymoon. But when I asked his wife if she was going to take a turn she said "No" instantly, adding that she felt it would feel too claustrophobic. Maybe I should have been more fearful about doing this, even in a swimming pool. I am sure my insurance forbids dangerous sports and this is probably on the list, but such activities have never been an issue in the past, as I have no ambition to make a parachute jump or eat raw fish an ill-judged bite of which can have you paralysed and in hospital in a trice. Here though if the tank had unaccountably been filled with some noxious gas that had curtailed both my holiday and also my life, my insurance would no doubt have proved null and void and my family would have been paying the cost of repatriating my body for the next ten years. Or maybe they could have just buried me on the hillside. Actually, if something like that should ever happen, I would be more than happy to stay put – go on people, save the repatriation money for a farewell party.

All too soon it was time to go. Our stay here had been wonderful, but we now had to fly back to Bangkok, and on to London. Somehow any difficulties encountered when travelling outward bound on a trip are more tolerable in the excitement of anticipation if the trip is intended to be a good one like a carefully planned or long anticipated holiday. It is always good to be homeward bound, however good a time you have had, and there are usually good things to be caught up with, family and friends not least amongst them. But the journey home is always more of a chore, even if everything goes smoothly.

Nevertheless it had to be done and we set off hoping that smoothly would be the right word to apply to it. Koh Samui airport was hot, the departure lounge was again an open sided building with a straw roof, but there were free drinks, soft seats and not too long to wait. The flight to Bangkok was good too. In Bangkok as we taxied in towards the terminal, we could see a gang of workers with yellow construction machinery resurfacing part of the runway. The airport's problems evidently continued. Then we were inside and had the labyrinthine corridors of Suvarnabhumi airport to traverse as we moved through to international and on towards our flight to London. After the one class flights to the island and back, here we sought the sanctuary of the executive lounge and hoped for smooth passage home.

It had been a wonderful trip. Nothing soured it like Harold had soured the flight that had prompted the idea. Burma was a truly new and special experience and I had experienced sights and sounds that would stay with me and remind me of it forever.

Chapter Fourteen

EPILOGUE

"Prediction is never easy. Especially of the future."
Neils Bohr

I am rarely conscious of dreaming; though I am told we all do it much of the night. But when I travel in a way that creates a marked time change, then on the nights I spend away I often remember dreams, even though such dreams are often pretty incoherent and fleeting. This journey was no different. Apart from dreaming of helping my now grown up daughter up some steps with her aged maybe six, I can remember none of it. However, on the final night at Napasai I woke having had a vivid dream. This time it remained clear in my mind as I got up. I had dreamt of the future and of our flight back to London.

This time the flight would arrive on time, and it would not circle for an hour because Heathrow's traffic controllers had unaccountably not realised it was coming and needed to land. This time even the slightest hiccup in landing would be accompanied by an intelligible and informative announcement that told us honestly what was happening, why and what the likely outcome was to be. This time when the flight home did land, taxiing would not cover a distance sufficient to take us into the next county. And we would draw up at a pier, not in some untidy, far flung wasteland of concrete where buses would first fail to appear, and then tour the entire airport before deciding where to deposit us. This time when we did reach a pier there would be someone there, someone already waiting to connect the plane to the door and allow the doors to be opened promptly. As we disembarked we would find ourselves not too far from the passport control counters, and any walkways en route designed to speed us on our way would actually be switched on and working. This time there would not be a queue of people of epic proportions waiting to have their passports checked, and the man in front of us would not present a passport that resulted in ten minutes of administrative unscrambling. In the baggage hall the sign would already display a clear and accurate indication of which luggage carousel our suitcases were destined to be disgorged onto and said suitcases would actually arrive, undamaged, before our jet lag escalated to the point where we fell asleep standing up. On this journey the taxi driver would be there on time as we walked out and we would find a luggage trolley that went forwards rather than pulling violently to the left or right. We would also not find ourselves gridlocked in the bowels of the multi-story car park by a car with foreign number plates entering along the going out lane. Finally, this time the motorway would not be in stationary chaos and we would get home before it was time for us to pack for the next trip.

Sadly of course this was only a dream. Did it come true? No. It. Did. Not. Pigs might fly, though those running Heathrow would not be likely to smooth their aerial ambitions either. Rather it provided proof, if proof were needed, that dreams usually have little or nothing to do with any accurate forecasting of the future and that sometimes you can learn from experience all too well. Actually the taxi driver did arrive on time, thank you Steve, but the less said about Heathrow in general and Terminal 3 in particular the better.

National embarrassment is nowhere near a strong enough description for London's "first" airport. This used to be a peculiarly British problem, but a while ago Britain's major airport was taken over by a large Spanish company. Why, I wonder? But we won't go there. But will someone sitting in Madrid be likely to care more than locally based management? I don't think it's a likely prospect, though given the prevailing chaos perhaps next time I travel through Heathrow I should expect to see one real improvement: a spanking new, super-efficient fast-track route through the check in process; for the exclusive use of those with a Spanish passport.

Negotiating the airport, back on home ground, may have been the least satisfactory part of the journey but eventually the Heathrow experience was left behind and forgotten and it did indeed prove good to be home.

What about Burma? Given the dire warnings about the Burmese government and my other various initial fears about visiting the country, was I pleased to have made the trip? Would I go again? Well, during the journey I did receive one firm prediction that I would return.

I mentioned earlier that a fortune teller was available one evening during the voyage on the *Road to Mandalay*. I had booked a session with him. The fortune teller, who told me his name was Saya Lwin, sat at a table on the upper deck. Beyond him the lights shone on the water and twinkled on the hillside like sparkling crumbs scattered for the birds. I looked out away from the ship for a moment while he did whatever preparatory magic was necessary having collected my details, date of birth and so on. Having consulted his various charts he told me I was born on a Tuesday, for which the linked animal is the lion and the predominant characteristic is honesty. I had to take his word for that; it is a while ago and I honestly did not remember. He had a penetrating look, appearing to gaze deep behind my eyes as he began to talk. And talk he did, rapidly and with conviction for more than half an hour. He covered an extraordinary number of things, seeming to put no priority on any one area and seeming also to be equally adamant about the validity of every prediction he made. He said I should go on working, which is true enough given the state of my pension. He said I should go on travelling, but it is no great insight to recognise that someone visiting Burma is not on their first trip and may well travel regularly and intend to continue to do so. He said I would return to Burma and also assured me that I would not die in an air crash. Not even on Air Mandalay, I wondered, and resolved that should I ever find myself spinning towards the ground at an uncontrolled 500 miles an hour, my final words will be "Saya Lwin – you were wrong!"

He flattered me a little, told me, "You have dignity", and said it was good for me to keep a dog, but not a cat. I have neither currently, though I have had both in the past. The number seven, the colour white or light green, red roses and diamonds and jade were all good for me. Well, a substantial quantity of diamonds would certainly be welcome, as it would for most people. Some of his predictions were very precise: something I lost a few years ago will come back to me in December, though I racked my brains thereafter to try to think of anything significant I had lost. I made a note. I made a list. But December came and went and nothing came to mind. One thing: his predictions continued on well into the future. A warning to friends and relations now: I am apparently going to live well into my 90s. If he was right about nothing else, then I certainly hope that particular prediction will prove to be true, but I will not spend recklessly in anticipation of the good financial fortune he predicted soon, as it is surely possible that he is not infallible.

He was firm in his prediction not only about my travelling more, but also about my returning to Burma. I wonder. Given my fears, and especially given the regime that this country and its people exist under, was I pleased I went when I did? Well yes, certainly I was. To visit or not is, though, a difficult balance to assess. On the one hand tourists clearly put some money into the government purse and they seem not to spend much of it on things like hospitals and prison reform. On the other hand, visitors do other things too. They show its people that Burma is not forgotten, help provide employment and earnings for many people and carry desperately needed information to and fro. People there, however hard their lives may be in some respects, appeared to like to see and speak with foreigners. Perhaps their lot would be worse if Burma was even more isolated and even less contact occurred with the outside world. You must decide.

Was the fortune teller correct? Will I go back again? Well, my fears were mostly groundless. There were no encounters with tigers. I only saw one spider, and whether or not it was poisonous it didn't bite me. I saw no snakes and experienced no earthquakes, though, as I reported, there was one just after we left and another in England just after we got back. Most unusual that is, and it was 4.3 in intensity and damaged a number of homes in a coastal town on the English Channel; the epicentre was evidently under the sea. Is nowhere safe? There was no harassment by military or police; not even a difficult question or hold up at passport control. None of the other potential hazards were evident, in fact, but then the trip was set up to be special and indeed it was. So, on that basis I would love to return, but it would be good to think that a future visit could be made after some radical change has brought long awaited change to this beautiful land. Though unless something changes both inside and outside the country, I fear that may not be for a while. But you never know – or maybe Saya Lwin does know and positive change is coming. If so I would love to think he was correct, change and improvement in Burma remains a cause many people inside and outside the country can assist and I have added a postscript that adds something about certain events that have taken place since my journey.

I read somewhere I remember not, of a Portuguese setting out to describe his country and saying in halting English, "My country is very small, but very much." Well said; perhaps I can end by saying much the same. Burma is definitely very much – very, very much.

POSTSCRIPT: LOOKING AHEAD, LOOKING BACK

*"It is always easier to talk
about change than to make it."*
Alvin Toffler

My journey made Burma real for me. When I see any sort of news about it now (and there seems to be more and more) it affects me much more than in the past, when, if I am honest, most of such coverage I hardly noticed. So let me end with some thoughts about what has happened since my visit and take a glance also to the future.

The way in which it appears to be human nature to live in a world of wishful thinking and ignore certain realities never ceases to amaze me. In part this perhaps comes from so many people taking a short term view. If a volcano is silent and harmless for a while there will be a city alongside it and people living on its slopes in a very short time. Yet the likelihood is that it will blow its top again one day; though even a small puff of smoke may quickly bring a dose of realism. Similarly we are pretty well informed about plate tectonics but development continues apace in all the wrong places and then surprise tends to be one of the feelings expressed when the plates inevitably shift again and damage is done above. Weather prompts the same view. Storms are often called exceptional, but this description really only relates to the short term outlook, and in terms of geological time, the fact that something that bad has not happened within the last hundred years does not mean it will never happen again. We seem to forget just how different things have been in the past, it is only 7/8,000 years ago since we could walk from England to Holland, and worldwide sea levels have regularly shifted up and down as have temperatures. Perhaps managing the world differently would mitigate some of the natural disasters that occur on a regular basis at least to some extent, because occur they will.

Even so, when disaster strikes, while many people in the world may express quite unjustified surprise, many also express sympathy and very often that is expressed as practical help for those affected. And for many, especially the poor living in vulnerable places, there is no choice. When trouble comes lives can be lost, or be changed radically and perhaps for ever.

And Burma is a vulnerable place.

I have already mentioned earthquake damage and another hazard is tropical storms, which are called cyclones in this part of the world. On Friday 2nd May 2008, Burma found its delta hit by a particularly violent storm: the cyclone Nargis. Nargis is an Urdu word meaning a flower (a daffodil in fact) which seems an odd coice of name for something so horrendous. It hit the Ayeyarwady delta at its peak strength, not least destroying some 65% of the rice crop current at the time. From being able to export small quantities of rice people went to facing serious shortfall and starvation. It was the single worst natural disaster to hit the country in recorded history. In such an area figures are difficult to verify, but certainly deaths were probably more than 150,000; nearly 100,000 people died in the most affected town, Labutta. Damage was estimated as costing US$ 10 billion, though this makes it sound somewhat impersonal and such things are better measured in lost lives, homes, businesses and disrupted families as well as infrastructure such as roads, schools and hospitals.

Despite the devastation, the government were slow to act and slow too to accept international help; maybe if you regard having the sort of government that rules Burma as itself a natural disaster then Nargis can be regarded as small beer. Much criticism was levied at the government from overseas as other countries and governments tried to offer help much of which was initially refused; indeed there followed months of wrangling as the junta grudgingly admitted the severity of what had occurred and allowed (some) assistance to be provided, while international aid agencies and governments pushed for access. The details of this reaction will not be stated here, suffice to say that it does not make happy reading nor does it do anything to mitigate the opinion you probably already have of those holding power in Burma; quite the reverse in fact.

This all occurred after my visit to the country, described here, and I do not want to try to add a history of these events, but a flavour of it is relevant as you will see. I well remember BBC reporters expressing amazement on their arrival in Burma about how little relief seemed to be organised or occurring. Indeed much time and effort that could have been directed at something useful was spent in harassing reporters and trying to prevent the outside world from seeing the true extent of the damage and certainly from seeing the pitiful job being done to help the many thousands of people affected. The message that "everything is being coped with" ultimately proved a vain attempt to disguise what was going on and the

BBC and others did manage to inform the world of the real situation. Having visited the country so recently, I found all the news very upsetting.

One victim of the damage was *Road to Mandalay*. As bad luck would have it this was moored in Yangon when the storm struck. If it had been elsewhere, perhaps in Bhama up near the Chinese border and its most northerly stopping place, then all would have been well. As it was it took a serious beating. Not only was it exposed to extensive water damage, but it suffered serious structural damage. Even a massive teak elephant that lives on the observation deck was cracked. I remember reading about this and wondering if it would ever sail again. It was in car-accident terms a "write-off". In the aftermath of all the horrors of the cyclone a few months of hiatus followed. In some ways Burma is a small outpost of the company's widespread operations. It would surely have been very easy to collect the insurance and build a nice resort somewhere that would not present similar hazards and on-going logistical problems in future. But their commitment to Burma and their view of its being special is strong. Badly damaged *Road to Mandalay* might have been, but it was repairable.

Negotiations with insurance companies can be difficult. There always seem to be a hundred and one reasons why a claim does not quite meet the terms of what you thought was a simple and clear arrangement. Maybe I'm over cynical about such things, but a recent claim to my travel insurers took more than four months and many letters before a cheque was grudgingly sent; and, yes, it does matter Nat West people, your service was abysmal. Anyway here lengthy negotiations with the insurance company secured an arrangement that allowed a complete refit and repair, so it was done; and how. Even so it took most of a year. The work was done in Yangon and led by François Greck, a French born, Laos-based architect. It made work for many local craftsmen and the fitting and finishing created an ambiance in sympathy with local colours and styles and replete with traditional Burmese materials, carving and weaving. No effort appears to have been spared to get it right.

What about the staff and crew? Everyone was kept on the payroll throughout the period the repair took and, while this appears sensible, it is also to the credit of the company that they did this (I bet there is no employment law in Burma to protect people in such circumstances). It must have cost a great deal of money. But it means that the laid back captain is still in charge and the wonderful San is still mesmerising his charges with the sights, history and culture of his beloved country. If I am ever on that observation deck again even my tea might be poured by the same person. So now these cruises are again a regular part of the river scene, and so too is the work the company does along the way to help local people. Such activity must be carefully judged as nothing must be done that can be interpreted by officialdom as "political". Despite this, significant activity is carried out and, for instance, a free medical clinic has recently been opened in Bagan and its operation is supported by the company. Staff members tell of the pleasure of seeing local people able to make what is in some cases literally their first visit to a doctor in their life.

So, once again, this splendid vessel is providing visitors with an unequalled way to see the sights that Burma has to offer and get a feel for this extraordinary country as it makes its way along the river which George Orwell described as "huge and ocherous, glittering like diamonds" and passes through the dream landscape that makes this country such a delight to visit. Long may it continue to do so.

When I made the journey described here I was going against advice about travel (though for what I saw as good reasons). In most countries government and a host of others work to maximise the level of tourism and see this as both desirable and financially beneficial. Such places need to have something attractive to offer, of course: the words beautiful downtown Lagos or the thought of trekking in Afghanistan are unlikely to top tourist attractions for a while. However, there are very few places, certainly places that are attractive to visit, where a variety of people actively canvass against visiting as is the case with Burma; or was.

The prohibition original stemmed from something opposition leader Aung San Suu Kyi, universally known simply as "The Lady", said, though this was a little ambiguous and some always felt she had not intended such fierce opposition to be the norm thereafter. Furthermore, whilst this certainly affected things on the global stage, while travelling I found that many local people had never heard of the policy. What is more, when told, they reacted with disbelief. How could their mixing with people from around the world, earning some money from it and helping people appreciate and understand the situation in Burma be wrong, they wondered. It is, I suspect, a sign of how Burma has been that such messages are neither widely distributed nor clearly understood by those who did hear them.

Now things are changing (and let me be wholly serious for a moment).

In November 2010 the release of the opposition National League for Democracy (NLD) party's Aung San Suu Kyi from house arrest and Burma's first parliamentary poll in two decades gave grounds for hope of change (even though Western leaders dismissed the election as neither free nor fair). But let's hope; what is the old saying about a journey beginning with a single step?

Soon after her release, and amongst much no doubt that she wanted to do, Aung San Suu Kyi changed her stance on travel to Burma. In May 2011, her National League for Democracy party issued a formal statement about tourism. This makes it clear that there can be bad things linked to tourism. For instance, people have been evicted from their homes to make way for such developments as a hotel or golf course and compensation is not in the Generals' vocabulary. Such development is not regarded either as in any way needing to balance matters like development and tourism; for example, one major concern is the way development around the beautiful Inlay Lake has despoiled water quality. Many of those living by, and getting their livelihood from, the lake now have to get drinking water from elsewhere. This sort of thing is not obvious to a visitor. That said policy regarding travel to Burma has changed and Aung San Suu Kyi is quoted as saying:

> "The NLD would welcome visitors who are keen to promote the welfare of the common people and the conservation of the environment and to acquire an insight into the cultural, political and social life of the country while enjoying a happy and fulfilling holiday in Burma."

She further said, in an interview with *Lonely Planet*:

> "Foreign tourists could benefit Burma if they go about (their travels) in the right way, by using facilities that help ordinary people and avoiding facilities that have close links to the government".

Over the last few years many tour operators have refrained from offering trips to Burma. Now, in the light of this and other comment, this too is changing. One company that has not been active in this way until after Aung San Suu Kyi's comments is Travel Indochina; in fact this company has for the last decade observed the boycott on travel to Burma. Now they are adding Burma to the destinations featured in their brochures. Their Managing Director Paul Hole, who is based in Australia, said:

> "... we are now of the opinion that it is time to try a new strategy. We have always believed that exchanges through travel can be an important catalyst for change, and we no longer believe that a boycott is the way to affect positive political change which can improve the lives of the Burmese people. Rather, our experience has taught us that such a boycott denies foreigners the chance to gain a real insight into the social and political issues at play in Burma and robs the local people of a 'voice', an opportunity to express their beliefs and opinions to the outside world. Recent surveys of our loyal traveller community confirm that the overwhelming majority of these like-minded travellers agree with us[2] ...The party's (National League for

---

[2] This is a view based on considerable research.

Democracy) shift in policy concurs with our long-standing view that small-scale travel practised by responsible tour operators and informed travellers can bring many benefits to the people of Burma. Travel Indochina goes to great lengths to maximise the percentage of tour operations expenditure which goes directly into the hands of local people in Burma. We do this through the use of local suppliers such as ground handlers, guides and drivers; as well as patronising privately-owned-and-run hotels, restaurants, shops and market stalls. Our tour operations comply fully with prevailing Australian, EU and US policies and legislation on trade with Burma and wherever possible, we avoid the use of government-owned-and-operated hotels and services.

Travel Indochina's grass-roots approach to travel lends much needed support to struggling local economies in Burma and brings its warm, wonderful people into direct contact with people from the outside world, to whom they can tell their story."

There is a longer version of this statement on the company's website (you can see this at *www.travelindochina.co.uk* – click on Burma then Policy Statement). Now, of course, such a company has holidays to sell, but I believe the attitude reflected here is sincere. Having read this I spoke to Paul O'Brian in the company's U.K. office, recently returned from a visit to Burma himself, he struck me as passionate about the country and caring about how what the company and their customers did for the situation. As, of course do *Road to Mandalay's* operators; they too have an ethical policy statement to reflect their approach. If you want a prediction let me say that I believe travel to Burma will now increase; and if you fancy going, and in my view who would not, then do not leave it too long – it is worth seeing in its present state of development (sic), before there is a McDonalds on every corner. Currently you can view a temple, that elsewhere would have a dozen coaches parked outside, the air noisy with the clicks of innumerable cameras, virtually all on your own. And if you want to hire an English-speaking guide then it is possible to afford one just for you.

Things are beginning to change on the ground too. For those wanting, or needing, to travel in a simple, low cost fashion, there are an increasing number of small, family run guest houses, eating out is cheap and so too is local transportation: buses and trains. You can hire a bicycle for only a pound or so a day. In fact if you want to travel around really cheaply go by bike, carry some milk and live on the cheese it will have turned into after you have bounced your way to the next guest house on the rough roads. Similarly in the air: internal flights cost less than in the past, though I do hope that does not mean they are cutting corners on necessary maintenance.

As tourist numbers rise, and remember they are still tiny, it is Asians who are leading the way; those visiting from China, Malaysia, Thailand and around the region seem to have no qualms about doing so. There is a long way to go in terms of the way the country is run really changing and, of course, if you do visit some money (if only for visa, government tax and tickets to enter those archaeological sites administered by the state) does go to the government. Much however will go to ordinary people who really need it and who will also, by all accounts, enjoy seeing you. Some, not all, will even risk joking with you about international and political matters: one comment heard – "Your country rich," addressed to a European tourist, "because your banks hold all our Generals' money!" My experience certainly suggested to me that visitors, and thus a wider experience of the country being spread around the world are likely to have both immediate benefit to those working in tourism and allied businesses and maybe, just maybe, will also help create a climate in which on-going political change continues to move towards a better future.

Clearly many problems remain in this beguiling country and assistance is needed and appreciated. If you want to help, then various charities would love to hear from you. Action Aid has a current initiative in Burma as I write this, but the main charity is Burma Campaign U.K. and there are equivalents in other locations. You can contact them at:

Burma Campaign U.K., 28 Charles Square, London N1 – 6HT Telephone: 0207 324 4713. Their website is *www.burmacampaign.org.uk*

The Burma Campaign U.K. certainly took a dim view of the 2010 elections saying:

> "Burma's fake elections, held on 7 November 2010, were part of the dictatorship's much-criticised 'road-map to democracy' that has been condemned around the world as an attempt to entrench and legitimize military rule. The entire process was a sham. The elections brought in a new constitution, which contains many undemocratic measures including the military having an effective veto over decisions made by the new Parliament and government. It was designed to keep the dictatorship in power and has not brought any new freedom to Burma's people."

No great level of approval there then, and evidence that much remains to be changed before one can truly say that real progress away from the dire circumstances of the last many years is occurring.

We will all see and read more about Burma in the future: about its government, its people and about travel to it. Also symptomatic of the growing interest in Burma is the film *The Lady*. This is the story of Aung San Suu Kyi, her husband, who played a significant part in her life, and her difficult work towards democracy. Made by a top film maker, Luc Besson, and starring Michelle Yeong, a strong actress who numbers being a Bond girl amongst her accomplishments, it has received good reviews. Similarly a new biography, *The Lady and the Peacock* by Peter Popham (Rider, 2011) was recently published.

Although some visitors I met along the way seemed totally ignorant of anything about the country they visited, and indeed some even remain so after a visit, taking in only the most superficial picture of the place, most are deeply affected by seeing this extraordinary country and some of those are disposed to help. I believe that more people visiting the country in future can be one factor assisting the changes that are in train. On the one hand the junta seem to have no problem with shooting monks in the street even though they know pictures will circulate the world via the internet in moments; and much of the problem is, of course, behind closed doors. On the other hand people seeing Burma, people talking to Burmese people and those people seeing that interest and feeling just a little less cut off from the rest of the world, must surely be a positive factor (though, as I was firmly told at Burma Campaign U.K., this is by no means guaranteed or the complete answer).

One recent visitor, someone who has been there a number of times, told me recently that they were greeted by several people saying "Welcome to the new Burma". I am sure they did not mean the new and perfect Burma, but it is surely a good sign and certainly very much changed from what I saw.

The fact remains that Burma, its history, people, culture and sights are all utterly beguiling. If ever there was a place that deserves to secure its proper place in the world then this is it. I hope some of what I have written here may have made you smile, but I hope it has informed you a little too, albeit without going into the serious politics, and that some readers may even decide to visit the country themselves.

To end, perhaps I can do no better than repeat and extend the phrase I stole and quoted at the end of the last chapter as the somewhat pigeon English somehow makes it spot on: Burma is very much – very, very much.

About the Author

Patrick Forsyth has worked for many years as a business consultant and management trainer. Linked to this he is the author of innumerable articles and a long list of successful business and management, personal development, self-help and career books (for example, *Successful Time Management*).

In recent years his writing has expanded into broader areas. He has had a humorous book published about life in the office jungle, *Surviving Office Politics* (Marshall Cavendish) and, more recently, *Empty When Half Full*, a book that highlights and castigates unfortunate consumer messages has been described as "Hilarious". This is published by Bookshaker. In addition, he has had short stories published and also writes about writing for *Writing Magazine* for which he also pens a monthly column.

He first travelled to South East Asia more than twenty-five years ago, and has visited regularly – especially to Singapore, Malaysia and Thailand - for both work and pleasure ever since. His first book of travel writing - *First Class At Last!* – is a light-hearted account describing a journey on the Eastern & Oriental Express, the luxury train that runs from Singapore to Bangkok. This was well reviewed, one reviewer calling it "*...lively, witty and wry*". His third travel title is *Smile Because it Happened*, which focuses on Thailand.

He lives in the United Kingdom, in Maldon in Essex, where he writes looking out over the River Blackwater.

Acknowledgements

As befits a journey designed to be stylish all went pretty smoothly, though this was due in large part to assistance I received both before and during the journey. So, first and foremost thanks are due to Anna Nash, Karima Chebani and all the staff connected with *Road to Mandalay* in both the United Kingdom and Burma and to the staff and crew on board. Thanks also to Somsri Hansirisawasdi and Anuttra Kiangsiriat at the Oriental Hotel in Bangkok, and to various members of staff there especially Anakarna and Kaynee. Similarly to Phillipe Bissig at the Governor's Residence in Yangon, Franz Von Merhart and Louise Toye with regard to the Napasai Resort in Koh Samui. All helped make this journey possible, and special.

Writing needs some commitment, and I am grateful to various family and friends for their help, though I might worry about just why some of them suggested that I shut myself away from everybody and "get on with it". I would mention especially, my wife Sue, who accompanied me on this trip. Ernest Hemingway is reputed to have said, "Never go on trips with anyone you do not love". Good advice: she not only made the trip more fun but helped, as ever, during the whole process of producing this book. I would also include my children Jacqui and Anthony and their spouses, Mark and Jenny: all are a support and have promised to encourage the grandchildren to read this too in due course.

Additionally, Sue put up with the regular *shut up I'm concentrating* noises emanating from me at the computer even when they did not have a *please* in them, and she and Jacqui kindly read drafts of this book and made (mostly!) constructive suggestions. I continue to value the support and comments of my writing group friends: they are regularly subjected to my reading a variety of not-finally-formed-extracts and their comments are always useful too. As ever, thank you all. I guess I should also thank all those who bought copies of my travelogue, *First class at last!*, especially those people I know who not only bought a copy but also encouraged me to write more in the genre of travel.

Publishers can make or break a book. This one would not have been possible without the help of the publishing team, editorial and promotional; sincere thanks to Lucy and Joe.

Finally, in true award ceremony mode, I must also mention: Jack and Silvia, the best holiday companions in the world, Siripan, friend and guide in Thailand, and Chloe, Timothy, Phoebe, Lydia, Joseph, Fabian and Tilly; thanks to you all for being there.

Oh, and perhaps I should add Harold too. Whoever and wherever you are, you prompted the idea – though for the sake of every traveller who might otherwise find themselves next to you as I did, please, *please*, give up flying.

Mandalay

by Rudyard Kipling

By the old Moulmein Pagoda, lookin' eastward to the sea,
There's a Burma girl a-settin', and I know she thinks o' me;
For the wind is in the palm-trees, and the temple-bells they say:
"Come you back, you British soldier; come you back to Mandalay!"
Come you back to Mandalay,
Where the old Flotilla lay:
Can't you 'ear their paddles chunkin' from Rangoon to Mandalay?
On the road to Mandalay,
Where the flyin'-fishes play,
An' the dawn comes up like thunder outer China 'crost the Bay!

'Er petticoat was yaller an' 'er little cap was green,
An' 'er name was Supi-yaw-lat – jes' the same as Theebaw's Queen,
An' I seed her first a-smokin' of a whackin' white cheroot,
An' a-wastin' Christian kisses on an 'eathen idol's foot:
Bloomin' idol made o'mud –
Wot they called the Great Gawd Budd –
Plucky lot she cared for idols when I kissed 'er where she stud!
On the road to Mandalay...

When the mist was on the rice-fields an' the sun was droppin' slow,
She'd git 'er little banjo an' she'd sing "Kulla-lo-lo!"
With 'er arm upon my shoulder an' 'er cheek agin' my cheek
We useter watch the steamers an' the "hathis" pilin' teak.
Elephints a-pilin' teak
In the sludgy, squdgy creek,
Where the silence 'ung that 'eavy you was 'arf afraid to speak!
On the road to Mandalay...

But that's all shove be'ind me – long ago an' fur away,
An' there ain't no 'busses runnin' from the Bank to Mandalay;
An' I'm learnin' 'ere in London what the ten-year soldier tells:
"If you've 'eard the East a-callin', you won't never 'eed naught else."
No! you won't 'eed nothin' else
But them spicy garlic smells,
An' the sunshine an' the palm-trees an' the tinkly temple-bells;
On the road to Mandalay...

I am sick o' wastin' leather on these gritty pavin'-stones,
An' the blasted Henglish drizzle wakes the fever in my bones;
Tho' I walks with fifty 'ousemaids outer Chelsea to the Strand,
An' they talks a lot o' lovin', but wot do they understand?
Beefy face an' grubby 'and –
Law! wot do they understand?
I've a neater, sweeter maiden in a cleaner, greener land!
On the road to Mandalay...

Ship me somewheres east of Suez, where the best is like the worst,
Where there aren't no Ten Commandments an' a man can raise a thirst;
For the temple-bells are callin', an' it's there that I would be –
By the old Moulmein Pagoda, looking lazy at the sea;
On the road to Mandalay,
Where the old Flotilla lay,
With our sick beneath the awnings when we went to Mandalay!
On the road to Mandalay,
Where the flyin'-fishes play,
An' the dawn comes up like thunder outer China 'crost the Bay!

Also by Patrick Forsyth

First Class At Last! (a journey through South East Asia)

Smile Because it Happened (focussing on the land of smiles: Thailand)

And, rather different, the hilarious *Empty When Half Full,* castigating consumer communication that too often turns into amusing weapons of mass misinformation

Praise for *First Class At Last!*

"... lively, witty and wry"
Select Books

"Sick to death of budget airlines and cramped hotel rooms, Forsyth decides to blow the budget and take a long trip in luxury. While his writing is witty, it is hardly a revelation that things are more comfortable in first class. But, if you miss the days of the empire, agree with him that Belgium is boring and that everyone on cruises is horrible, then this will be a treat."
The Good Book Guide

"... witty and full of interesting facts"
Essex Life

"... it reminded me of Bryson..."
Neal Asher, bestselling author of *Gridlinked*

Lightning Source UK Ltd.
Milton Keynes UK
UKOW030203080412

190303UK00006B/11/P